Contents

Photographs: ADAC 66, 67; ADN Zentralbild (GDR) 37; Allsport 61; Austrian National Tourist Office 21, 62; Bundesministerium für das Post- und Fernmeldewesen 44; Bundesrepublik Deutschland – Fotodienst 10, 26, 27, 38, 43; Creditanstalt Bankverein 12; Deutsche Bundesbahn 18, 19, 47; Deutsche Grammophon Production 60; Embassy of the German Federal Republic 4, 47, 66; Fremdenverkehrsverband für Wien 36, 47; German National Tourist Office 7, 30, 47, 77; Bob Hallmann front cover, 12, 22, 26, 29, 31, 35, 41, 44, 45, 47, 55, 57, 64, 67, 68, 72; Imperial War Museum 7; Inter-Nationes 10, 12, 13, 18, 21, 25, 32, 54; Karstadt 49, 71; Kaufhof 31; Landeshauptstadt Düsseldorf 47; Lufthansa 14; Mansell Collection 6, 76; Rod and Sonja Nash 4, 5, 10, 12, 13, 15, 17, 18, 19, 20, 21, 22, 23, 24, 25, 26, 27, 28, 29, 30, 31, 33, 34, 35, 36, 37, 38, 39, 40, 41, 42, 43, 44, 45, 47, 48, 49, 52, 53, 56, 57, 58, 59, 64, 65, 66, 67, 69, 70, 71, 72, 73, 74, 75, 76, 77; Panorama DDR 19, 21, 23, 48, 68, 69; Pictorial Press 61; Paul Popper 7, 60; Press Association 60; Duncan Prowse 35, 44, 49, 66; Jürgen Schadeberg back cover, 9, 20, 48, 52; Jamie Simson 8, 9; Sporting Pictures 5, 60; David Streeter/Schools Abroad 40; Tony Stone 40; Raimund Vornbäumen 42.

What do you know about Germany?

Guten Tag!

Guten Tag. Ich heiße Gabi Müller, und ich wohne in Dortmund — das ist in der Bundesrepublik Deutschland. I'm going to tell you a lot about my country, to help you prepare and enjoy your stay with us. I shall also show you glimpses of other countries where German is spoken. Can you name any of them?

Can you find Dortmund on a map? It's on the edge of the Ruhrgebiet, the big industrial area of West Germany.

Hi! I'm Bob! I learn German at school in Britain. We're going to Germany soon so I must start getting organised. I'm really excited!

The traffic-free shopping centre in Dortmund.

Quick Quiz

Let's see what you know already.

1 Here are five countries where German is spoken, and their capital cities. Which capital belongs to which country?

Land	*Hauptstadt*
West Germany	Vienna
East Germany	Bonn
Austria	Vaduz
Switzerland	East Berlin
Liechtenstein	Bern

The **Bundeshaus**, beside the river in Bonn. This is where the **Bundestag** (equivalent of the House of Commons) meets. Do you know the name of the river?

2 Here are the five flags of the countries in question 1. Which flag belongs to which country?

A   B   C   D   E

3 Here are the international registration plates of the five countries. Which plate belongs to which country?

4 Here are some famous sports personalities from German-speaking countries. Which country does each of them come from? Who does which sport?

Steffi Graf
Michael Groß
Heike Drechsler
Bernhard Langer
Katharina Witt
Peter Müller

A Athletics
B Golf
C Tennis
D Skiing
E Swimming
F Skating

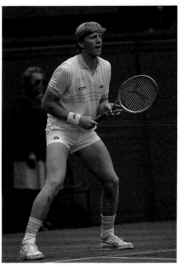

Right: In 1985 Boris Becker was the youngest player ever to win the Wimbledon Tennis Championship. Do you remember how old he was? Which country does he come from?

Do remember ...

DO remember that cars drive on the right.

DO wait at pedestrian crossings until your light is green. You can be fined on the spot if you are caught crossing when the light is red.

DO try lots of different foods and drinks. This boy is trying **Wiener Backhendl** (chicken baked in bread crumbs). Do you fancy it?

DO write down new words and phrases. Try and write them down in the context you heard or read them; this will help you remember them.

DO try and speak as much German as you can. Nobody minds if you make mistakes.

DO collect things for a souvenir album – for example tickets, stamps, postcards, brochures, beer mats, wrappers.

Which of these tickets is for:

1 a football match?
2 a boat ride on a lake?
3 a visit to the zoo?
4 climbing to the top of a cathedral?
5 parking?

Which countries are the tickets from?

Look at the currencies:

West Germany = **Deutsche Mark**
East Germany = **Mark**
Austria = **Schilling**

Germany past

Many states become one nation

Germany? No such place!

The original Germanii were tribes from Scandinavia, in about 1,000 B.C. Many of them moved south into central Europe. By the Middle Ages there were over 350 states. Most were within the sphere of influence of the Austrian Habsburg Empire. The Holy Roman Emperor, appointed by the Pope, made sure they remained faithful to him and to Rome. The idea of a country called Germany did not exist.

Luther and reform

In 1517 the priest Martin Luther (born 1483) nailed his treatise against the corruption of the Catholic church to the door of the **Schloßkirche** (Castle Church) in Wittenberg. In doing so he shook not only the authority of the Pope, but that of the Emperor too. Luther's Protestant Reformation spread to such an extent that a

hundred years later, Germany was plunged into the Thirty Years War (1618-48), between the Protestant North and the Catholic South. This war reduced the population by 35 per cent, and the number of states to 234.

Prussia: the military state

The War left Germany poor and ravaged. The **Junker**, the Protestant landowners of Prussia, turned to their military prowess as the only way to prosper. Frederick the Great, King of Prussia (1712-86), was a composer, flautist and friend of the French philosopher Voltaire. But he is remembered as a general, who spent two thirds of Prussia's revenue on his conscript army; defeated both France and Austria (with finance from England) in the Seven Years' War (1756-63); and who enlarged Prussia into a major European power.

Bismarck: the skilled statesman who guided the Germans towards unity.

German unification

All over Europe in the eighteenth century, thinkers such as **Montesquieu, Rousseau, Goethe** and **Kant** were exploring new ideas about society. The French revolutionaries took up many of these new ideas. The victorious French armies spread the doctrine of nationalism: the unity of people with a common language and culture.

At the end of the Napoleonic wars, Germany was still divided into many small states, some in the Austrian sphere of influence, some in the Prussian. Liberal thinkers wanted a free, united Germany. Instead, unity was provided by the military regime of Prussia. Under its Chancellor, **Otto von Bismarck**, Prussia disposed of the Austrian challenge by occupying Vienna in the six-week Austro-Prussian war of 1866. France was defeated in 1871. From Versailles, Bismarck declared the existence of the new German Empire.

Frederick the Great: highly cultured and very warlike.

Trench warfare: one of the greatest horrors of World War I.

Empire and expansion

When **Wilhelm II** (William II) became Emperor in 1888, he soon dismissed Bismarck and set out on a policy of military and imperial expansion. The German Empire was to rival the British and French Empires world-wide. Germany was already a strong industrial power with 50 million people. The vain and unstable William was not the man to control the situation. He found himself propelled by the extremist and power-hungry military establishment into confrontation with Britain, France, Russia and Austria. Complex military and political alliances criss-crossed Europe. The German navy grew larger and larger. Finally the spark that ignited the fire of all the international rivalries was provided in June 1914 by the assassination of the heir to the Habsburg throne. In August 1914 the German military machine swung into action. In the four years of World War I, eight and a half million people were killed and 21 million wounded.

Defeat ... and war again

Germany emerged from World War I crushed – physically and morally. Vast reparations were due by the Treaty of Versailles to repay France for war damage. Money had been borrowed to pay for the war, and the politically unstable **Weimarer Republik** (Weimar Republic) faced huge inflation – a sackful of money was needed to buy daily food – and mass unemployment. In this tense atmosphere **Adolf Hitler** tried to launch a revolt against the government in Munich in 1923. In prison afterwards he set out in **Mein Kampf** (My Struggle)

his three basic beliefs: the superiority of the Aryan race; the evils of Communism; and the guilt of the Jews for Germany's defeat in World War I. A great orator, he played on German national pride, and with the support of industrialists who wanted Germany to rearm, he became Chancellor in 1933. From then on the Nazis – members of the **Nationalsozialistische Deutsche Arbeiterpartei** (National Socialist German Workers' Party) took over every aspect of the state.

Hitler and his Nazis were megalomaniacs. They thrust Germany into a new world war in which 55 million people died, among them 18 million Russians and almost five million Germans. Six million Jews were killed in concentration camps. After the War Germany was occupied by the Allies, and has been divided ever since.

Cologne in ruins from bombing during the war. Inset: post-war reconstruction.

Germany present

The nation is divided again

A view from West Berlin over the graffiti-covered Wall.

Divided by the Allies

At the end of World War II, Germany and Austria were divided into four **Besatzungszonen** (zones of occupation): French, Russian, British and American. Berlin, situated well inside the Russian zone, was similarly divided.

In May 1949 the three Western zones were formed into **Die Bundesrepublik Deutschland,** with Bonn as its capital and Konrad Adenauer as its first **Bundeskanzler** (Federal Chancellor – equivalent of our Prime Minister). The Russian zone had gone its own political and social way, and in October 1949 was declared the **Deutsche Demokratische Republik**, part of the Communist bloc. From 1961 Berliners were prevented from leaving East Berlin by the construction of the **Berliner Mauer** (Berlin Wall) which now divides the city into East and West Berlin.

In 1955 Austria became an independent republic again.

Recovery

After the war, the Western Allies were determined to help West Germany to recover. The currency reform of 1948, the spirit of the West German people, and the dollars provided by America's Marshall Plan sparked off the **Wirtschaftswunder** (Economic Miracle) that has made West Germany into one of the most prosperous nations in the world. Germany's rapid post-war expansion was helped by immigrants from Turkey, Italy and Yugoslavia, who came to work in German factories.

Industry has revived in East Germany too. It is now one of the world's ten leading industrial nations, although the shops are not so well stocked as in West Germany. East Germany has to export to pay its way.

Government in the BRD

The West Germans have two votes, one for a local candidate and one for a political party.

Thus half of the **Bundestag** is elected by proportional representation. A party has to get five per cent of the votes before it is assigned **Abgeordnete** (Members of Parliament). The **Bundespräsident** (Federal President) has a comparable role to that of the British monarch. The main political parties are:

CDU: Christlich-Demokratische Union (Conservatives)

CSU: Bavarian equivalent of CDU

SPD: Sozialdemokratische Partei Deutschlands (Labour)

FDP: Freie Demokratische Partei (Liberals)

Grüne: The Greens (Ecology party)

In 1983, for the first time, an ecology party achieved over five per cent of the votes. After the general election in January 1987 the Greens had 42 of the

8

Immigrant workers in West Germany are called **Gastarbeiter** (guest workers). They and their families take lessons in German.

503 **Abgeordnete**, and with the **SPD** they formed the official opposition to the governing **CDU/CSU/FDP** coalition. Their supporters are concerned about nuclear power, pollution and the consumer society.

Government in the DDR
The **DDR** has five main political parties, but the **Sozialistische Einheitspartei Deutschlands – SED –** has been in power since the end of the War and is by far the most important. The present **Generalsekretär** (General Secretary) of the **Volkskammer** (Parliament) in East Berlin is Erich Honecker.

Divisions in Berlin
The isolated, divided city of Berlin, the old capital of Prussia, became the heart of the Cold War. Hot war threatened in 1948, when the Russians tried to cut West Berlin off from the world with a year-long blockade. The building of the Wall in 1961 revived tension.

In the 1970's Chancellor Willi Brandt tried to ease East-West tension. His **Ostpolitik** (policies towards the East) led, for example, to West Berliners being allowed to phone and visit relatives in East Berlin.

Because West Berlin is so cut off, being in the middle of East Germany, many people are reluctant to settle there. But it is a very busy, lively city, which provides entertainment of all kinds; and young people in particular enjoy living there.

Divided in the future?
In 1966, 28 per cent of Germans thought that it was unlikely that East and West Germany would ever be re-united. In 1980, 52 per cent held that view. The East-West divide has separated many families; but it seems likely that East and West Germany will remain two different countries.

Below left: Checkpoint Charlie, a crossing point between East and West Berlin.
Right: the post-1945 division of Germany and of Berlin.

Where are you going?

There's so much to see!

Ich heiße Matthias. Ich bin Gabis Cousin aus Lübeck.

Es ist Spitze hier an der Nordsee!

Ich bin Gabis beste Freundin Nicole.

Sommerferien mit Freunden auf der Nordseeinsel Juist – das Wetter war herrlich!

Hier sind einige Fotos aus meinem Album.

The scenery in German-speaking Europe is varied, and often very beautiful. The map below shows the main geographical features.

Das Ruhrgebiet, wo ich herkomme (oben); und das idyllische Dorf Schönbach in Österreich.

Nordsee
Ostsee
NIEDERLANDE
Lüneburger Heide
DDR
POLEN
Berlin
Ruhrgebiet
Harz
Elbe
Sauerland
Sächsische Schweiz
Westerwald
Thüringer Wald
Erzgebirge
BELGIEN
Eifel
Rhein
BRD
CSSR
LUXEMBURG
Bayerischer Wald
FRANKREICH
Schwäbische Alb
Donau
Schwarzwald
Wienerwald
Salzkammergut
SCHWEIZ
Alpen
ÖSTERREICH Tauern
Alpen
Alpen
ITALIEN
JUGOSLAWIEN
LIECHTENSTEIN

German-speaking Switzerland

This page from a diary gives holiday dates.

Schuljahr 1987/88

Land	Sommerferien von	bis	Herbstferien von	bis	Weihnachtsferien von	bis
Baden-Württemberg	2.7.	15.8.	26.10.	30.10.	24.12.87 Winterferien: 15.02.88	5.1.88 19.02.88
Bayern	30.7.	14.9.	keine	*)	23.12.87	9.1.88
Berlin	9.7.	22.8.	3.10	10.10.	23.12.87	6.1.88
Bremen	29.6.	8.8.	5.10.	10.10.	23.12.87	9.1.88
Hamburg	18.6.	1.8.	5.10	17.10.	21.12.87	2.1.88
Hessen	19.6.	31.7.	5.10	9.10.	21.12.87	8.1.88
Niedersachsen	25.6.	5.8.	1.10.	10.10.	23.12.87	6.1.88
Nordrhein-Westfalen	16.7.	31.8.	26.10.	31.10.	23.12.87	6.1.88
Rheinland-Pfalz	23.7.	2.9.	19.10	24.10.	23.12.87	9.1.88
Saarland	23.7.	5.9.	26.10	31.10.	21.12.87	4.1.88 ***)
Schleswig-Holstein	18.6.	1.8.	5.10	17.10.	23.12.87	6.1.88

*) am 2. und 3.11.1987 ist schulfrei
**) am 13.5.1988 ist schulfrei
***) Fastnacht 15.2. - 16.2.88

Where will *you* be?

Look at both the maps. Can you find the spot where you will be?
- Which **Land** will you be in?
- What is the nearest big town?
- Will you be near a border or a major river?

There are 11 **Länder** in West Germany: the eight in italics on the map above, plus Hamburg, Bremen and West Berlin.

There are nine **Länder** in Austria: the eight in italics, plus Vienna (which is also the capital city of **Niederösterreich**).

There are 15 **Bezirke** in East Germany, named after their capital cities.

In Switzerland the regions are called **Kantone**. Seventy-five per cent of the Swiss speak **Schwyzerdütsch** (Swiss German). What other languages are spoken there?

To prevent too much chaos on the roads, the different **Länder** in West Germany stagger the dates of their school holidays. Look at the dates for 1987/88 (see chart on the left):
- Which **Land** breaks up for its summer holidays first?
- What is special about Baden-Württemberg?
- What is different about the autumn half-term holiday in Hamburg and Schleswig-Holstein?

Who speaks German?

Look how many people speak German:
BRD: 61 Millionen
DDR: 17 Millionen
Österreich: 7 Millionen
Schweiz: 4 Millionen
Liechtenstein: 18 000 Tausend

Even some people in Luxembourg, France and Italy speak it! But though the written language is the same, the dialects in the spoken language are so strong that a North German finds it difficult to understand a Bavarian, an Austrian or a Swiss speaking **Schwyzerdütsch**. Sometimes even the words are different. Look at this list of North German and Austrian differences (some of the Austrian words are heard in South Germany too).

Norddeutschland	*Österreich*
GutenTag!	**Grüß Gott!**
Auf Wiedersehen	**Auf Wiederschauen**
Junge	**Bub**
Treppe	**Stiege**
Januar	**Jänner**
dieses Jahr	**heuer**
zu Hause	**daheim**
gucken	**schauen**

Most people will speak standard German **Hochdeutsch** with you. But see if you can discover any local dialects or words on your trip.

Let's find out more

Go into your local travel agent's – they may be able to give you some leaflets. And drop a line to the **Verkehrsamt** (Tourist Information Office) in the nearest big town to where you will be. Ask them to send you some information. Use this model letter.

Cardiff, den 4. März

Sehr geehrte Damen und Herren,

In sechs Wochen fahren wir mit unserer Klasse nach Wiesbaden.

Wir würden uns sehr freuen, wenn Sie uns einige Prospekte über Wiesbaden und Umgebung zusenden könnten.

Wir danken Ihnen im voraus für Ihre Mühe.

Mit freundlichen Grüßen,
Andy Sparrow

Packed and ready to go!

Money

West German notes and coins. How many **Pfennig** are there in a **Mark**?

Austrian **Schilling** and **Groschen**. How many **Groschen** are there in a **Schilling**?

> *Weißt du, wie das Geld aussieht?*

You can buy your foreign currency before you leave, or on the ferry, or abroad. You may want to take **Reiseschecks** (traveller's cheques) with you. These can be refunded if lost, but must be ordered in advance.

When you need a bank, look for the signs shown here, or ask people: „**Wo ist die nächste Bank?**"

Kassenstunden
von 8³⁰ bis 13⁰⁰ Uhr
von 14³⁰ bis 16⁰⁰ Uhr
donnerstags bis 17³⁰ Uhr
samstags sind unsere Kassen geschlossen

RAIFFEISENKASSE
Geldwechsel
Exchange
Change
Cambio
Travellers
Cheques

What time does the bank above open?
Does it shut for lunch?
On which day is it open later?
Is it open on Saturdays?
How does all this compare to bank opening times in Britain?

Übung macht den Meister

> *Ich möchte 10 Pfund umtauschen, bitte.*

> *Und ich möchte für 20 Pfund Reiseschecks einlösen, bitte.*

How would you ask to change the following:
1 £5?
2 £12?
3 £15?
4 £10 traveller's cheques?
5 £25 traveller's cheques?
Look for the exchange rate in the paper. How many **DM** will you get for a pound?

How many **Schilling** will you get for a pound?

You won't find the rate for East German marks as you can't buy them in the West.

Are you sure you've packed everything?

> Here's my luggage list. I hope I haven't forgotten anything!

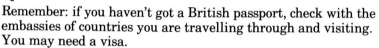

Paß	Geld/Reiseschecks
Hemden	Versicherung
Pulli	Fotoapparat
Schuhe	Unterwäsche
Anorak	Kuli/Schreibpapier
Jeans/Hose	Adreßbuch
Notizbuch	Wörterbuch
Socken	Toilettenartikel
	Sonnenbrille

Match the correct name to each object. Then make your own list.

Remember: if you haven't got a British passport, check with the embassies of countries you are travelling through and visiting. You may need a visa.

If you're going to West Germany, get a form E111 from your local Social Security office. This tells you how to get free medical treatment in Common Market countries.

What will the weather be like?

Here is the weather forecast taken from a German newspaper. What sort of weather can be expected today in North Germany? In South Germany? In Switzerland? In Austria?

What were the hottest towns in Europe yesterday?

Make a list of the towns mentioned. Can you write next to them *in German* the countries they are in?

What will you add to your luggage list if you go skiing?

Going to the DDR

If you travel by road to West Berlin, you'll need a transit visa to cross East Germany.

If you travel from West to East Berlin for a day, you'll have to change 25 **DM** into East German **Mark**, which have to be spent before you return.

Few people spend holidays in East Germany, but it is an interesting country to visit. The State travel agency, called Berolina, in London, does all the booking for you. You can stay in hotels, luxurious but very expensive, or on camp sites. Everything must be booked in advance. Visas can be acquired in London, and you change your money at the border.

East German notes are smaller and the coins lighter than West German ones.

DAS WETTER

Ein Hochdruckgebiet über den britischen Inseln verlagert seinen Schwerpunkt nach Polen und führt trockene Festlandluft nach NRW. Morgens Dunst, örtlich auch Nebel, der sich rasch auflöst, tagsüber sonnig und Erwärmung auf 22 – 26°.

WEITERE AUSSICHTEN:
Sonnig, trocken und noch etwas wärmer.

SO SIEHT ES IN EUROPA AUS:
Norddeutschland: Überwiegend sonnig, 24 – 27°
Süddeutschland: Vorübergehend sonnig, einzelne gewittrige Schauer, 22 – 26°
Dänemark: Heiter bis wolkig, 22 – 25°
Beneluxländer/Frankreich: Wolkig mit Aufheiterungen, einzelne Schauer oder Gewitter, 22 – 27°
England/Irland: Im Süden noch heiter bis wolkig, sonst veränderlich stark bewölkt und Regen, 14 – 19°
Spanien: Heiter bis wolkig, einzelne Gewitter, 25 – 30°
Österreich/Schweiz: Im Osten vielfach sonnig, im Westen überwiegend starke Bewölkung, einzelne Gewitter, 22 – 27°
Italien/Korsika/Balearen: Teils sonnig, teils wolkig, einzelne Schauer oder Gewitter, 24 – 28°
Kanarische Inseln: Heiter bis wolkig, 25 – 27°
Wassertemperaturen: Nord- und Ostsee: 19 – 21°, Schwarzes Meer: um 23°, Kanarische Inseln: um 22°, westl. Mittelmeer: 24 – 26°, östl. Mittelmeer: 24 – 27°

GESTERN (13 UHR):	
Berlin	heiter 20°
Nordern.	heiter 20°
List	heiter 17°
Hamb.	heiter 20°
K.Asten	heiter 16°
München	bewölkt 19°
Kopenh.	heiter 21°
Hoek	bewölkt 16°
Prag	heiter 20°
London	bedeckt 16°
Paris	heiter 18°
Wien	bewölkt 23°
Budap.	bewölkt 27°
Zürich	Regen 18°
Brest	heiter 19°
Nizza	bewölkt 26°
Split	bedeckt 25°
Bukar.	heiter 27°
Rom	Regen 26°
Athen	heiter 30°
Barcel.	heiter 22°
Palma	bewölkt 27°
Palmas	heiter 24°
Tunis	heiter 30°
Moskau	bewölkt 11°

IM REVIER:
Essen (13 Uhr): 16°, heiter, Max. 22°, Min. 13°

VOR EINEM JAHR:
Essen (13 Uhr): 18°, wolkenlos, Max. 22°, Min. 10°

How do we get there?

We're going by sea

Vergiß nicht deine Reisetabletten!

The best way to travel will depend on where you live in Britain.

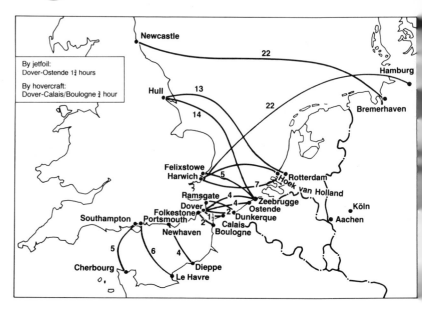

By jetfoil:
Dover-Ostende 1½ hours

By hovercraft:
Dover-Calais/Boulogne ¾ hour

Sea crossings: some routes with numbers of hours.

Most young people visiting Europe travel overland; and that means crossing the North Sea or the English Channel. The map shows some of the crossings you can take.

If you go by coach or car, which crossing will mean least driving in Britain?

Which crossing will mean least driving on the Continent?

What are the advantages and disadvantages of the longer crossings in terms of time, money and convenience?

If you go by train, make sure you're in the right carriage – the trains often divide up in Europe. You will see your carriage destination written on the side.

Check in advance whether you have to change trains.

What is your train's final destination?
Has the train got a name?

I'm glad I'm not down there in all that traffic!

I hope we can fly!

Look at the photo: near which airport was the photo taken?

Do you think the plane is landing or taking off?

How many types of transport can you see in the picture?

The speed limit on a West German **Autobahn** (motorway) is normally 130 km/hr. But this limit is only *recommended*, not compulsory.

On a map, find all the towns on the road signs.

The plane belongs to the West German airline **Lufthansa**.

Übung macht den Meister

1	`06·00`
2	`09·15`
3	`11·30`
4	`13·05`
5	`15·25`
6	`19·45`

You may have to put your watches forward an hour when you reach the Continent. You can check on the boat or plane.

Practise telling the time. Start with the times on the clocks on the right and the 24-hour times on the left.

Wie spät ist es?
Wieviel Uhr ist es?
If you want to know the time, ask either of these questions.

Make sure you can understand the 24-hour clock. It is used much more on the Continent than in Britain.

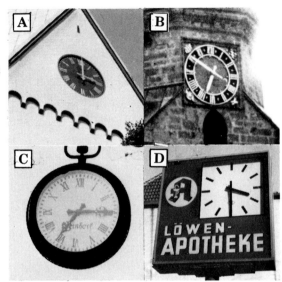

Crossing the Rhine

> *Wenn du über die Autobahn oder mit dem Zug fährst, wirst du wahrscheinlich unseren größten und berühmtesten Fluß, den Rhein, überqueren.*

The Rhine's source is in Switzerland, and 1,320 km later (867 of them in West Germany) it flows into the North Sea in the Netherlands.

It is of major economic importance to West Germany as it provides a transportation link between the South, the industrial Ruhr and the North Sea.

The castles, picturesque towns and vineyards of the Middle Rhine between Bonn and Bingen attract thousands of tourists.

OPEN-AIR FESTIVALS

6. 6.: **BERLIN** Reichstags-Gelände – David Bowie & Guests

6. 6.: **NÜRBURGRING** – Eurythmics, Bruce Hornsby, Bob Geldof, UB 40, Echo & The Bunnymen, Chris Isaak, Stan Ridgeway, Clowns & Helden u. a.

7. 6.: **NÜRBURGRING** – David Bowie, The Smiths, Gianna Nannini, Udo Lindenberg, Andy Summers, H. R. Kunze, China Crisis, Ina Deter u. a.

7. 6.: **BERLIN** Reichstags-Gelände – Eurythmics, Bruce Hornsby u. a.

27. 6.: **MÜNCHEN** Galopp-Rennbahn Riem – Chris de Burgh, Bob Geldof, China Crisis u. a

28. 6.: **MÜNCHEN** Galopp-Rennbahn Riem – Tina Turner, Joe Cocker, Eurythmics. Robert Cray u. a

2. 7.: **BERLIN** Waldbühne – Tina Turner, Joe Cocker u. a.

3. 7.: **HAMBURG** Volksparkstadion – Tina Turner, Joe Cocker, Eurythmics u. a.

4./5. 7.: **ESSEN** Georg-Melches-Stadion – Tina Turner, Joe Cocker, John Farnham

7. 7.: **BERLIN** Waldbühne – Jimmy Cliff, Third World. U-Roy u. a.

10. 7.: **BERLIN** Waldbühne – Siouxsie & The Banshees, Iggy Pop, Mission, Julian Cope u. a.

11. 7.: **LORELEY** Freilichtbühne – Siouxsie & The Banshees, Iggy Pop, Mission, New Model Army u. a.

One of the little castles on the Rhine, the Pfalz near Kaub. Can you see the pleasure boat? What does the **H** stand for on the bus stop?

> *So this is why they call it "rock music"!*

One of the many legends about the Rhine concerns a beautiful girl who sang so sweetly on the **Loreley** rock that the sailors below forgot about navigating, and were shipwrecked and drowned! Nowadays the music sounds a little different since the **Loreley** is famous for the **Open-Air-Festivals** held there every year. Look at the extract from **Bravo** (a teenage magazine). Do you know any of the groups playing?

15

Getting about by car

Where's that car from?

Guten Tag! Ich möchte euch Deutschlands Straßen zeigen. Was für ein Wagen bin ich? Woher komme ich?

Here are the symbols of five other makes of German car. Can you link the correct name to each symbol? ▶

In West Germany it's easy to tell where a car is from. Just look at the first letter(s) on the registration plate and consult the chart below. You will see other registrations, but they are being phased out. **HH** stands for **Hansestadt Hamburg**.

Mercedes

Opel

Audi

BMW

Volkswagen

1
2
3
4
5

The **Hansestädte** were a group of North German trading towns who combined in the Middle Ages to protect their economic interests overseas (and fought trade wars with Denmark and England).

Unterscheidungszeichen der Verwaltungsbezirke

a) Gültige Unterscheidungszeichen *)

A
A	Augsburg
AA	Ostalbkreis in Aalen
AB	Aschaffenburg
AC	Aachen
AIC	Aichach-Friedberg in Aichach
AK	Altenkirchen Westerwald
AM	Amberg
AN	Ansbach
AÖ	Altötting
AS	Amberg-Sulzbach in Amberg
AUR	Aurich
AW	Bad Neuenahr-Ahrweiler in Ahrweiler
AZ	Alzey-Worms in Alzey

B
B	Berlin
BA	Bamberg
BAD	Baden-Baden
BB	Böblingen
BC	Biberach, Riß
BGL	Berchtesgadener Land in Bad Reichenhall
BI	Bielefeld
BIR	Birkenfeld Nahe
BIT	Bitburg-Prüm in Bitburg
BL	Zollernalbkreis in Balingen
BM	Erftkreis in Hürth
BN	Bonn
BO	Bochum
BOR	Borken in Ahaus
BOT	Bottrop
BRA	Wesermarsch in Brake Unterweser
BS	Braunschweig
BT	Bayreuth
BÜS	Konstanz, Gem. Büsingen/Hochrh.

C
CE	Celle
CHA	Cham
CLP	Cloppenburg
CO	Coburg
COC	Cochem-Zell in Cochem
COE	Coesfeld
CUX	Cuxhafen
CW	Calw.

D
D	Düsseldorf
DA	Darmstadt
DAH	Dachau
DAN	Lüchow-Dannenberg in Lüchow
DAU	Daun
DEG	Deggendorf
DEL	Delmenhorst
DGF	Dingolfing-Landau in Dingolfing
DH	Diepholz
DLG	Dillingen a. d. Donau
DN	Düren
DO	Dortmund
DON	Donau-Ries in Donauwörth
DT	Lippe in Detmold
DU	Duisburg
DÜW	Bad Dürkheim Weinstraße in Neustadt Weinstraße

E
E	Essen
EBE	Ebersberg
ED	Erding
EI	Eichstätt
EL	Emsland in Meppen
EM	Emmendingen
EMD	Emden
EMS	Rhein-Lahn-Kreis in Bad Ems
EN	Ennepe-Ruhr-kreis in Schwelm

ER	Erlangen
ERB	Odenwaldkreis in Erbach Odenwald
ERH	Erlangen-Höchstadt in Erlangen
ES	Esslingen Neckar
ESW	Werra-Meißner-Kreis in Eschwege
EU	Euskirchen

F
F	Frankfurt/Main
FB	Wetteraukreis in Friedberg Hessen
FD	Fulda
FDS	Freudenstadt
FFB	Fürstenfeldbruck
FL	Flensburg
FN	Bodenseekreis in Friedrichshafen
FO	Forchheim
FR	Freiburg
FRG	Freyung-Grafenau in Freyung
FRI	Friesland in Jever
FS	Freising
FT	Frankenthal Pfalz
FÜ	Fürth

G
GAP	Garmisch-Partenkirchen
GE	Gelsenkirchen
GER	Germersheim
GF	Gifhorn
GG	Groß-Gerau
GI	Gießen
GL	Rheinisch-Bergischer Kreis in Bergisch-Gladbach
GM	Oberbergischer Kr. in Gummersbach
GÖ	Göttingen
GP	Göppingen
GS	Goslar
GT	Gütersloh in Rheda-Wiedenbrück
GZ	Günzburg

H
H	Hannover
HA	Hagen
HAM	Hamm
HAS	Haßberge in Haßfurt
HB	Hansestadt Bremen
HD	Heidelberg
HDH	Heidenheim Brenz
HE	Helmstedt
HEF	Hersfeld-Rotenburg in Bad Hersfeld
HEI	Dithmarschen in Heide-Holstein
HER	Herne
HF	Herford in Kirchlengern
HG	Hochtaunuskreis in Bad Homburg vor der Höhe
HH	Hansestadt Hamburg
HI	Hildesheim
HL	Hansestadt Lübeck
HM	Hameln-Pyrmont in Hameln
HN	Heilbronn
HO	Hof
HOL	Holzminden
HOM	Saar-Pfalz-Kreis in Homburg/Saar
HP	Bergstraße in Heppenheim Bergstraße
HR	Schwalm-Eder-Kreis in Homberg
HS	Heinsberg in Erkelenz
HSK	Hochsauerlandkreis in Meschede
HU	Main-Kinzig-Kreis in Hanau
HX	Höxter

I
IGB	St. Ingbert
IN	Ingolstadt
IZ	Steinburg in Itzehoe

K
K	Köln
KA	Karlsruhe
KB	Waldeck-Frankenb. in Korbach
KC	Kronach
KE	Kempten (Allgäu)
KEH	Kelheim
KF	Kaufbeuren
KG	Bad Kissingen
KH	Bad Kreuznach
KI	Kiel
KIB	Donnersbergkreis in Kirchheimbolanden
KL	Kaiserslautern
KLE	Kleve
KN	Konstanz
KO	Koblenz
KR	Krefeld
KS	Kassel
KT	Kitzingen
KU	Kulmbach
KÜN	Hohenlohekreis in Künzelsau
KUS	Kusel

L
L	Lahn-Dill-Kreis in Wetzlar
LA	Landshut
LAU	Nürnberger Land in Lauf a. d. Pegnitz
LB	Ludwigsburg
LD	Landau
LER	Leer in Leer Ostfriesland
LEV	Leverkusen
LG	Lüneburg
LI	Lindau (Bodensee)
LIF	Lichtenfels
LL	Landsberg a. Lech
LM	Limburg-Weilburg in Limburg Lahn
LÖ	Lörrach
LU	Ludwigshafen Rhein

M
M	München
MA	Mannheim
MB	Miesbach
ME	Mettmann
MG	Mönchengladbach
MH	Mülheim a. d. Ruhr
MI	Minden-Lübbecke in Minden
MIL	Miltenberg
MK	Märkischer Kreis in Lüdenscheid
MM	Memmingen
MN	Unterallgäu in Mindelheim
MOS	Neckar-Odenwa Kreis in Mosbach
MR	Marburg, Bieden kopf in Marburg Lahn
MS	Münster
MSP	Main-Spessart in Karlstadt
MTK	Main-Taunus-Kr. in Hofheim am Taunus
MÜ	Mühldorf a. Inn
MYK	Mayen-Koblenz in Koblenz
MZ	Mainz
MZG	Merzig-Wadern in Merzig Saar

N
N	Nürnberg
ND	Neuburg-Schro hausen in Neub a. d. Donau
NE	Neuss
NEA	Neustadt a. d. Aisch-Bad Wind heim in Neustad a. d. Aisch
NES	Rhön-Grabfeld Bad Neustadt a. d. Saale
NEW	Neustadt a. d. Waldnaab
NF	Nordfriesland in Husum
NI	Nienburg Wese
NK	Neunkirchen Sa
NM	Neumarkt i. d. C
NMS	Neumünster
NOH	Grafschaft Bent in Nordhorn
NOM	Northeim
NR	Neuwied Rhein
NU	Neu-Ulm
NW	Neustadt Weins

O
OA	Oberallgäu in Sonthofen
OAL	Ostallgäu in Marktoberdorf
OB	Oberhausen
OD	Stormarn in Bad Oldesloe
OE	Olpe

On the motorway

The first **Autobahnen** in Germany were built in 1928 (when were the first ones built in Britain?). Hitler did a great deal to extend the network. Today you can travel all across German-speaking Europe by motorway.

The sign on the far right tells you that you are approaching a border. Which border? And what facilities are available at the service station?

The other sign welcomes you when you cross the border into West Germany. It gives you the compulsory and recommended speed limits. Which do you think is which? How do the German speed limits compare with the British ones?

Make sure you can change kilometres into miles! Remember, 8 kilometres = 5 miles. So to get miles, divide the number of kilometres by 8 and multiply by 5.

How many miles are:

1 16 km? **2** 24 km? **3** 50 km? **4** 64 km?
5 96 km? **6** 100 km? **7** 130 km?

Practise using this chart by identifying German cars.

Offenbach, Main	**SC**	Schwabach	**VEC**	Vechta	
Ortenaukreis in Offenburg	**SE**	Segeberg in Bad Segeberg	**VER**	Verden in Verden Aller	
Ostholstein in Eutin	**SFA**	Soltau-Fallingbostel in Fallingbostel	**VIE**	Viersen	
Osterode Harz	**SG**	Solingen	**VK**	Völklingen	
Osterholz in Osterholz Scharmbek	**SHA**	Schwäbisch Hall	**VS**	Schwarzwald-Baar-Kreis in Villingen-Schwenningen	
Oldenburg/ Oldenburg	**SHG**	Schaumburg in Stadthagen			
Osnabrück	**SI**	Siegen			
	SIG	Sigmaringen	**W**		
P	**SIM**	Rhein-Hunsrück-Kreis in Simmern	**W**	Wuppertal	
Passau	**SL**	Schleswig-Flensburg in Schleswig	**WAF**	Warendorf in Beckum	
Pfaffenhofen a. d. Ilm	**SLS**	Saarlouis	**WEN**	Weiden i. d. Opf.	
Rottal-Inn in Pfarrkirchen	**SO**	Soest	**WES**	Wesel in Moers	
Paderborn	**SP**	Speyer	**WF**	Wolfenbüttel	
Peine	**SR**	Straubing	**WHV**	Wilhelmshaven	
Pforzheim	**ST**	Steinfurt	**WI**	Wiesbaden	
Pinneberg	**STA**	Starnberg	**WIL**	Bernkastel-Wittlich in Wittlich	
Plön Holstein	**STD**	Stade			
Pirmasens	**SU**	Rhein-Sieg-Kreis in Siegburg	**WL**	Harburg in Winsen Luhe	
	SÜW	Südliche Weinstraße in Landau	**WM**	Weilheim-Schongau in Weilheim i. Ob.	
R					
Regensburg	**SW**	Schweinfurt			
Rastatt	**SZ**	Salzgitter	**WN**	Rems-Murr-Kreis in Waiblingen	
Rendsburg-Eckernförde in Rendsburg			**WND**	St. Wendel	
Recklinghausen in Marl	**TBB**	Main-Tauber-Kreis in Tauberbischofsheim	**WO**	Worms	
			WOB	Wolfsburg	
Regen			**WST**	Ammerland in Westerstede	
Roth	**TIR**	Tirschenreuth			
Rosenheim	**TÖL**	Bad Tölz-Wolfratshausen in Bad Tölz	**WT**	Waldshut in Waldshut-Tiengen	
Rotenburg Wümme					
Remscheid					
Reutlingen	**TR**	Trier	**WTM**	Wittmund	
Rheingau-Taunus-Kreis in Rüdesheim	**TS**	Traunstein	**WÜ**	Würzburg	
	TÜ	Tübingen	**WUG**	Weißenburg-Gunzenhausen in Weißenburg i. Bay.	
Ravensburg	**TUT**	Tuttlingen			
Rottweil					
Herzogtum Lauenburg in Ratzeburg	**U**		**WUN**	Wunsiedel i. Fichtelgebirge	
	UE	Uelzen			
	UL	Ulm Donau	**WW**	Westerwald in Montabaur	
S	**UN**	Unna			
Stuttgart					
Schwandorf	**V**		**Z**		
Saarbrücken	**VB**	Vogelsbergkreis in Lauterbach Hessen	**ZW**	Zweibrücken	

Arriving at a town

When you arrive at a town, you see a sign giving the name of the town. The speed limit immediately becomes 50km/hr. When you leave a town, you pass a sign with the name crossed out. This means you can increase speed.

Have you heard of Colditz? It is in East Germany, between Leipzig and Karl-Marx-Stadt. Its castle was used as a top security prison in the Second World War. There were many exciting attempts to escape. It is no longer a prison.

Arriving . . .

. . . and leaving.

Colditz Castle. What is it used for today?

Travelling by train

Signs at the station

> Es ist ziemlich teuer, mit der Bahn zu fahren — aber so entspannend!

This train is an Intercity travelling along the Rhine valley near St. Goarshausen.

When you want to buy a ticket, look for signs saying **Fahrkarten** or **Fahrausweise**. Just say how many tickets you want (**einmal**, **zweimal** etc), the town you are visiting, and whether you want your ticket **einfach** (single) or **hin und zurück** (return).

These symbols tell us where you can do various things. Should these people go **links** (left) or **rechts** (right)?

A > Ich möchte Geld umtauschen.

B > Ich habe Hunger. Ich möchte etwas essen.

C > Ich muß unbedingt zur Post.

D > Ich habe meine Fahrkarte noch nicht gekauft.

E > Ich weiß nicht, wann der nächste Zug nach Bonn fährt.

Frankfurt am Main station is one of the largest and busiest in West Germany.

Types of trains

S-bahn: Stadtbahn: A town train.
Nahverkehrszug: A local train, stopping at most stations.
E-Zug: Eilzug – rather quicker, stopping at fewer stations.
D-Zug: Durchgehender Zug: A fast train. You'll have to pay a **Zuschlag** (supplement) unless you travel at least 50 km.
Intercity: Again, a **Zuschlag** has to be paid.
TEE: Trans-Europa-Express – first class only, and *very* expensive.

On an East German train.

Übung macht den Meister

Einmal Freiburg hin und zurück, bitte.

80,- DM, bitte.

With a partner, practise asking for your ticket. Your partner can tell you what it costs.

The timetable

Departures from Dortmund.

There are two timetables displayed in German stations: **Ankunft** (arrival times) and **Abfahrt** (departure times).

Look at the extract from the departure timetable in Dortmund **Hbf** (**Hauptbahnhof**- main station). Which three types of train are mentioned?

Which train would you take if you wanted to get to Cologne quickly?

How long does the journey to Munich take?

Which platform do you need if you want to go to Mönchengladbach?

All set for the off!

You've got your ticket, so go on to the platform. Where will you get to if you follow this sign?

Zugang zu den Gleisen 2-5

The indicator will confirm that you are on the right platform. What platform are the people in the photo on?

What time does the train leave?
What sort of train is it?
Will a supplement have to be paid?
What is the train's final destination?

Schauen Sie auf die Anzeigetafel.

German-speaking cities

West Germany's top ten

Stadt		Einwohner
1	Berlin (West)	1 902 000
2	Hamburg	1 653 000
3	München	1 300 000
4	Köln	976 000
5	Essen	652 000
6	Frankfurt am Main	628 000
7	Dortmund	610 000
8	Düsseldorf	595 000
9	Stuttgart	582 000
10	Duisburg	559 000

West German cities according to their population.

Find the top ten cities on a map. How many of them are in the South of Germany?

How many are in the **Ruhrgebiet**?

Will you be staying near one of these cities?

Which rivers flow through or near the cities?

Which is your nearest big town in Britain, and how does it compare in size?

The port is the heart of Hamburg.

Six famous cities

Hamburg

Hamburg is probably more famous for its water than its land. It is the most important port in West Germany, with 20,000 ships arriving and departing every year. Hamburg is also West Germany's second largest industrial city (after West Berlin), and an important printing town, with 4½ million newspapers being produced there every day. It also has a famous football team.

München

Many consider Munich the most beautiful town in West Germany. It is the capital city of **Bayern** (Bavaria), an important agricultural area which extends down to the German Alps. The Bavarians consider themselves somewhat apart from the rest of Germany, especially from the "Prussian North". They even have their own border posts (right).

Dresden

One of the most beautiful cities in the **DDR**, Dresden was heavily bombed at the end of the last war and has been painstakingly rebuilt. Two of its most impressive buildings are the **Kulturpalast** (Civic Centre), and the **Zwinger**, a palace which also had to be rebuilt after 1945 and which houses many fine collections of art and pottery.

Karl-Marx-Stadt

The town of Chemnitz was also rebuilt after the war, and in 1953 was renamed Karl-Marx-Stadt after the man who, with Friedrich Engels, founded Communism.

Wien

The capital of Austria, Vienna is a city of music, theatre, good food, beautiful parks and the world famous Spanish Riding School. It also owns many of the treasures of the Habsburgs, the old rulers of the Austro-Hungarian Empire.

Salzburg

Salzburg, just across the Austrian border, is a lovely city dominated by the **Festung** (castle). Since 1920 Salzburg has become world famous for its **Festspiele,** a summer festival of music.

The stadium at Munich was built for the 1972 Olympics.

Es gibt hier so viele schöne Städte. Schreib etwas über alle, die du besuchst.

Quick Quiz

1 Which of the cities on these two pages hosted the 1972 Summer Olympics and the 1974 Football World Cup?
2 Which is famous for its boys' choir?
3 Which gets its name from the salt mines nearby?
4 Which are located on the Elbe River?
5 Which provided the beaten finalists in the 1987 European Cup football championship?
6 Which famous composers are associated with Vienna?
7 Which famous composer was born in Salzburg?

Inside the Zwinger Palace, Dresden.

Lipizzaner horses of the Spanish Riding School: they are born black, but grow grey.

Sculpture of Marx in Karl-Marx-Stadt.

The **Festung** and churches of Salzburg.

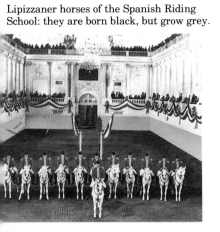

21

Settling in

What kind of room?

Die Hotels sind nicht so teuer bei uns!

There are all sorts of rooms to be had everywhere.

If you are going to stay in a hotel or guest house find out:

- its name and address
- its telephone number
- the code for phoning it from Britain

Of course, the better the facilities, the more you'll have to pay. These symbols are from a hotel guide. Which symbol goes with which explanation?

A **Doppelzimmer ohne Bad/Dusche**

B **Doppelzimmer mit Bad/Dusche**

C **Einzelzimmer ohne Bad/Dusche**

D **Restaurant**

E **Lift**

F **Parkplatz**

G **Zimmertelefon**

1 2 **R**

3 ↑↓ 4

5 **P** 6 ☎

7

I like youth hostelling!

Es macht Spaß, in einer Jugendherberge zu übernachten; man lernt so viele Leute kennen.

West Germany has 572 **Jugendherbergen** (youth hostels), Austria has 129 and Switzerland 89. People from many countries stay in them, as they provide a cheap and friendly way of travelling. Some youth hostels even have family rooms. If you're going to stay in a youth hostel, don't forget your **Mitgliedsausweis** (membership card).

A youth hostel in the Sauerland. On the left: the signs for West German hostels (above) and East German hostels (where people from the West cannot stay).

Übung macht den Meister

When you reach the place where you're going to stay, you'll want to find out where various things are. Match these drawings to the correct name, then with a partner practise asking where the things are.

> *Entschuldigen Sie, bitte.*
> *Wo ist das Badezimmer?*

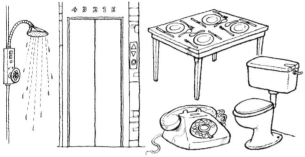

1 die Dusche   2 die Toilette   3 das Eßzimmer
4 das Telefon   5 der Lift

Was meinst du?

In the next two pages you'll see what life is like in a typical German home.

What do you think are the advantages and disadvantages of:
● staying in a hotel?
● staying in a youth hostel?
● camping?
● staying with a family?

What suggests that this camp site is in East Germany?

Extra++ extra++ extra++

> *I like camping best... But if I go to a hotel, I must be able to ask the right questions!*

| *Wann schließt das Hotel abends?* |
| *Um wieviel Uhr gibt es Frühstück?* |
| *Wo ist der Frühstücksraum?* |
| *Verkaufen Sie Ansichtskarten vom Hotel?* |
| *Kann man zu jeder Zeit duschen?* |

> *I hope your hotel is more welcoming than this one in Burghausen!*

> *Lecker!*

> *Schmeckt furchtbar, das Essen!*

A meal provided by a youth hostel. A few hostels have kitchens where you can prepare your own meals.

In a German home

Write a letter

If you're going on an exchange trip, it's a good
idea to write a short letter first – like this one.

Heinz sent me this photo
of himself at home before I
did an exchange with him.

Bedford, den 8. April

Liebe Bärbel!

Ich bin Deine Austauschpartnerin und freue
mich sehr auf die zwei Wochen bei Dir.

Ich heiße Ros, bin 14 Jahre alt und wohne
in einer Mietswohnung. Wo wohnst Du? Ich habe
einen Bruder Gary, er ist zwei Jahre älter als
ich.

Was machst Du gern in Deiner Freizeit? Ich
spiele gern Tennis, schwimme gern und höre gern
Musik. Mein Lieblingssänger ist Prince.

Schreib mir alles über Dich und Deine
Familie.

Schöne Grüße,
Ros

In a family

What will it be like staying
with a German family?

There will be a lot of hand-shaking, including
when you go to bed and when you get up.

Remember to call a child **du** and an adult **Sie**.

Don't expect a hot breakfast. You might get **ein
gekochtes Ei** (a boiled egg), but otherwise
Germans eat **Brot** (bread) or **Brötchen** (rolls),
Aufschnitt (cold sliced meats), **Käse** (cheese),
Marmelade (jam) and **Butter**. The usual drinks
are **Kaffee, Kakao** or **Milch**. Can you label all
the things on this breakfast table? They include
Quark, which is a curd cheese, and a bowl of
Leberwurst (liver sausage).

Because German pupils start school so early,
they often have a **zweites Frühstück** at break.
What do you think it is?

Before starting to eat, people will probably wish
you „**Guten Appetit**"; you reply „**Danke,
gleichfalls!**" ("And you too!").

If you take a **Gastgeschenk** (present brought
by a guest) with you for the family, here are a few
typically British things: tea, shortbread, pottery,
picture books about Britain, and souvenir
sweat-shirts.

Your own home

Fast die Hälfte aller westdeutschen Familien besitzen ein Eigenheim.

Flats with a children's playground, in West Germany. On the left: a house in Salzburg, in Austria. Notice the **Fensterläden** (shutters).

Since the last war many new homes have been built, and many old ones renovated. A third of the population of West Germany lives in large towns, usually in rented flats. In East Germany too, most people live in flats. Rents are particularly cheap there.

The cellar makes the difference!

Houses in Germany are usually more spacious than they look because most have a cellar. Even flats have a small cellar for storage in the basement of the block. The **Reihenhaus** (terraced house) in the photo has a large cellar.

There are four rooms in the cellar. One contains the heating equipment, another has a washing machine and tumble dryer. The third is a guest room, and the fourth is a store room containing supplies of drink, tinned foods, fruit and vegetables, and a **Gefriertruhe** (freezer). Part of the contents of the store room are shown in the drawing on the right and the photos below. Make a list of the things in German.

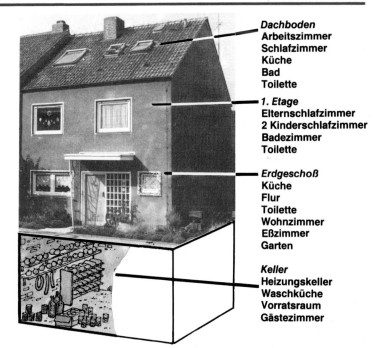

Dachboden
Arbeitszimmer
Schlafzimmer
Küche
Bad
Toilette

1. Etage
Elternschlafzimmer
2 Kinderschlafzimmer
Badezimmer
Toilette

Erdgeschoß
Küche
Flur
Toilette
Wohnzimmer
Eßzimmer
Garten

Keller
Heizungskeller
Waschküche
Vorratsraum
Gästezimmer

In the country

Enjoying the countryside

Grüß Gott, ihr da unten! Ist diese Landschaft nicht herrlich?

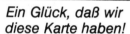

Ein Glück, daß wir diese Karte haben!

Toll — der kann das gut!

The Germans love **Radfahren** (cycling), especially when it's not too hilly. They need the hills when the snow comes, though. **Skilaufen** (skiing) and **Rodeln** (tobogganing) are very popular.

„Mein Vater war ein Wandersmann"

This is the first line of a famous German song. Do you know what the song is called in English?

Wandern (hiking) is very popular, especially at the weekend.

Many areas have boards showing routes for **Wanderwege**

nach	über	Zeichen	Zeit	Beginn
Herdecke	Olpketal–Viermärker Eiche–Wittbräucke–Sonnenstein	▣	5 Std.	Kaiser-Hain
Schloß Hohenlimburg	Wannebachtal–Hohensyburg–Hengsteysee–Bad Henkhausen	✕	6½ "	
Wetter	Auf dem Blick–Ende–Drei Buchen–Haus Schede	▭	6 "	Westfalenhal (Steinerner Tu
Hohensyburg	Tierpark–Olpketal–Höchsten–Wannebachtal	△	3½ "	
Hohensyburg	Brücherhof–Gut Niederhofen–Höchsten–Wannebachtal	◈	3 "	Hörde Brückenplat
Westhofen	Brücherhof–Höchsten–Wannebachtal–Gut Kückshausen	▢	3¼ "	"
Witten	Viermärker Eiche–Auf dem Schnee–Appelsiepen–Hohenstein	▤	5 "	Jugendherb Höchsten
Unna	Sommerberg–Freischütz–Eichholz–Opherdicke	▤	5 "	"

(country hikes). These tell you how long a walk takes, and which signs you should follow.

Look at the board above. Whic sign should you follow for the shortest of the hikes shown?

How long will the hike to Herdecke take?

Where is the starting point for the hike to Witten?

Down on the farm

What crops can I expect to see growing in the countryside?

Over 50% of West Germany is farm land. Here are some of the most important crops. Which drawing goes with which name?

Getreide

Obst

Weintrauben

Kartoffeln

Gemüse

Hopfen

In East Germany most of the farm land is worked by cooperatives: groups of farmers, known as **Landwirtschaftliche Produktionsgenossenschafter** (**LPG**'s). The farms are much bigger than in the West, and some of the fields are enormous!

This **Mähdrescher** (combine harvester) is at work near Halle in East Germany.

What about a glass of wine?

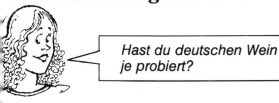

Hast du deutschen Wein je probiert?

A small part of the selection of wines in a German supermarket. The wines are grouped by area.

West Germany has only one per cent of the world's wine producing area, and yet its wines are famous the world over.

Austria too produces fine wines, mainly in the East of the country south of Vienna. Will you be staying near a wine-producing region?

Rhein wines are sold in brown bottles, **Mosel** in green. The **Franken** wines are in distinctive, flask-shaped bottles, known as **Bocksbeutel**.

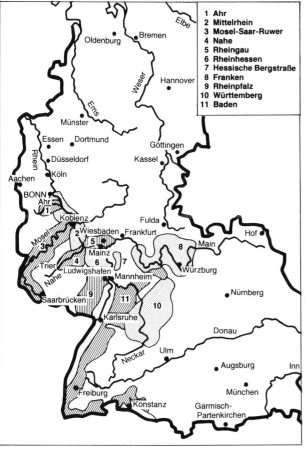

1	Ahr
2	Mittelrhein
3	Mosel-Saar-Ruwer
4	Nahe
5	Rheingau
6	Rheinhessen
7	Hessische Bergstraße
8	Franken
9	Rheinpfalz
10	Württemberg
11	Baden

The eleven wine-growing regions of West Germany.

Schau dich um

When you are in Germany:
- See if people drink more wine or more beer.
- Find out where the wines come from.
- Look at the prices. Is wine expensive there?
- Find out which have been the best years for wine recently and why.
- Collect labels from wine bottles, like these. Which wine-growing areas do they come from?

Here the **Weinlese** (harvest) is still done by hand, but it is often done by mechanised grape-pickers.

Wir sind fast fertig!

I'll show you round the town

Übung macht den Meister

This is the centre of Freiburg, a beautiful university town in the **Schwarzwald** (Black Forest). Imagine you are standing on the star ✳ facing north. With a partner, practise asking the way to various places on the map.

> Entschuldigen Sie, bitte. Wie komme ich zur Universitätskirche?

> Ganz einfach. Geh hier geradeaus, dann die erste rechts, und die Kirche ist sofort links.

1 Münster 2 Kaufhaus 3 Wenzingerhaus 4 Rathaus 5 Universitätskirche 6 Universität 7 Martinstor 8 Schwabentor

Getting around

Like many German cities, Karl-Marx-Stadt in East Germany still has **Straßenbahnen** (trams).

Only one British city still has trams. Do you know which it is?

West German trams often carry advertisements, but there is little advertising in East Germany because there is little private enterprise and therefore no need to compete for custom.

Buses are popular too. But you'll see double deckers only in West Berlin.

If you travel by bus or tram, you often get your ticket in advance, as they don't have conductors. So look out for ticket machines or stands. When you're on the bus you stick your ticket in an **Entwerter** (cancelling machine) which punches it.

A tram in Karl-Marx-Stadt, East Germany. (Can you remember the old name of this city?)

The monorail in Wuppertal.

The town of Wuppertal lies stretched out along a river valley (which river is it?). At the turn of the century they built a **Schwebebahn** (monorail) to make transport easier. They once carried a baby elephant in it to advertise the famous Wuppertal zoo! Unfortunately it panicked, charged and jumped through the doors, and landed (unhurt) in the river below.

The Rathaus and the Verkehrsamt

The **Rathaus** and the **Marktplatz** in the old university town of Tübingen.

Look out for these places.

A tourist trying to repeat the mayor's feat.

In the photo above you can see two people acting the mayor of Rothenburg and his daughter. Every year, the city celebrates the time when the mayor's daughter begged attacking enemies not to sack the city. They agreed – provided that a citizen could drink a 3-litre pot of wine at one draught. The mayor did so.

Most towns have a **Rathaus** (town hall). The photo on the cover was taken outside the **Rathaus** in Cochem. The **Brunnen** (fountain) is a popular meeting point for teenagers. What do you think of their clothes?

Look for Cochem on a map. Which river is it on? Can you remember why this river is famous?

Go into the **Verkehrsamt** when you visit a German town. They will give you a street plan and information about the town and what you can do there.

The brochure provided by the **Verkehrsamt** in Rothenburg shows symbols for things to do there. Which symbol goes with which entertainment?

1 **Museum**
2 **Reiterhof**
3 **Fluß zum Angeln**
4 **Tennisplatz**
5 **Kunstausstellung**
6 **Wanderweg**
7 **Kegelbahn**
8 **Freibad**
9 **Flugplatz**
10 **Golfplatz**
11 **Hallenbad**
12 **Kinderspielplatz**

Practise asking your way to these places.

Extra++ extra++ extra++

Here are some of the questions you may want to ask at the **Verkehrsamt**. What do they mean? Practise using them before you go.

Haben Sie einen Stadtplan?

Was gibt es hier in der Umgebung zu sehen?

Sind diese Prospekte kostenlos?

Was gibt es hier für junge Leute zu tun?

Entschuldigen Sie, bitte. Wie komme ich am besten zum Rathaus?

Komm mit!

Let's go shopping

Shopping is different

German shops are open longer than ours – and not all of them close for lunch like the one in the photo on the right. However, except on **der lange Samstag** (the first Saturday of the month), the shops are closed on Saturday afternoons.

What does the word **Eingang** mean? And what is the advertisement on the door for?

To avoid traffic congestion, some big towns provide free coaches which take shoppers from car parks outside the city, then back again when they've done their shopping.

Shopping for souvenirs in the **Fußgängerzone** (pedestrian precinct) in Heidelberg.

In East Germany

Many East German shops have the letters **HO** on them, standing for **Handelsorganisation**. They are run by the State. Basic requirements, such as food, are relatively cheap in East Germany; but "luxury" items, such as fashionable clothes, tend to be expensive. If you pay in Western currency, you can purchase Western goods in **Intershops,** which are official State shops selling Western goods. The people who shop there are either Westerners or East Germans who have obtained the currency through relatives living abroad.

What can you buy in these two shops?

Übung macht den Meister

If you buy fruit or vegetables in Germany, you will ask for them in **Kilo** (kilograms) and, in some parts of the country, in **Pfund** (pounds). **1 kg = 2 Pfund**. Yet 1 kg is equivalent to 2·2 English pounds; so is a German **Pfund** slightly heavier or lighter than an English pound?

Bitte schön?

Ein Pfund Tomaten und ein Pfund Birnen, bitte.

With a partner practise ordering fruit and vegetables from the market at Leipzig (on the right). Your partner should write down the quantity you ask for.

What can you buy where?

FERNSEH HIFI VIDEO *Hallmann*

BÜCHER KRÜGER

What can you buy in these shops?

Hier ist meine Einkaufsliste — wo kann ich diese Sachen kaufen?

Einkaufsliste

12 Brötchen
2 Kalbsschnitzel
Hustenbonbons
Farbfilm
Videokassette
Deutsch-englisches Wörterbuch

- **Fleischerei** and **Metzgerei** are the same.
- If you need a chemist be careful, because there are two types: in an **Apotheke** you will get mainly medicines, cough sweets etc. This is also where you take any prescriptions. If you need soap, toothpaste, tampons, tissues etc, go to a **Drogerie.**

In a department store

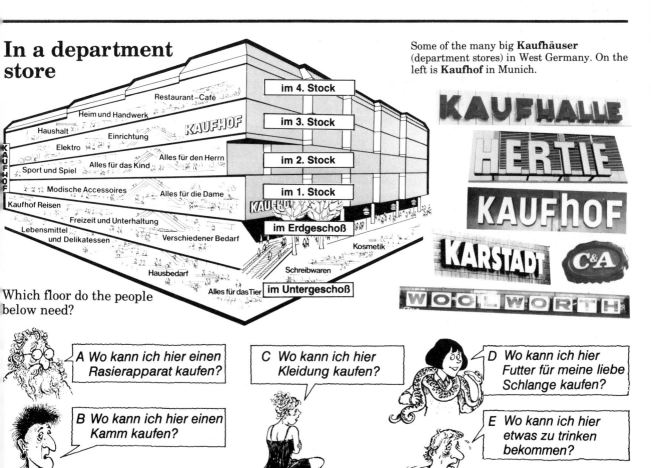

Some of the many big **Kaufhäuser** (department stores) in West Germany. On the left is **Kaufhof** in Munich.

im 4. Stock — Restaurant–Café

im 3. Stock — Heim und Handwerk / Haushalt / Einrichtung

im 2. Stock — Elektro / Alles für den Herrn / Sport und Spiel / Alles für das Kind

im 1. Stock — Modische Accessoires / Alles für die Dame / Kaufhof Reisen

im Erdgeschoß — Freizeit und Unterhaltung / Lebensmittel und Delikatessen / Verschiedener Bedarf / Kosmetik

im Untergeschoß — Hausbedarf / Schreibwaren / Alles für das Tier

KAUFHALLE HERTIE KAUFhof KARSTADT C&A WOOLWORTH

Which floor do the people below need?

A Wo kann ich hier einen Rasierapparat kaufen?

B Wo kann ich hier einen Kamm kaufen?

C Wo kann ich hier Kleidung kaufen?

D Wo kann ich hier Futter für meine liebe Schlange kaufen?

E Wo kann ich hier etwas zu trinken bekommen?

31

I know a good restaurant

We enjoy eating out

> *Das deutsche Essen ist herzhaft und reichlich. Es stimmt nicht, daß wir immer nur Würstchen essen!*

The Germans enjoy eating out, and you will find a wide range of restaurants to choose from.

The beer mat on the right shows a picture of an old building which used to be a hospital and is now a restaurant.

Nuremberg is famous for its spicy sausages. Look at the menu below: on what sort of plates are the sausages served? What comes with them? How are they prepared?

Wein-Groß-Gaststätte
HEILIG-GEIST-SPITAL
NÜRNBERG (an der Museumsbrücke)
Günter Leitner
Gesellschaftsräume
20–100 Pers.
Weine auch im Straßenverkauf

Where in Nuremberg is this restaurant?

Speisekarte

Vom offenen Buchenholz-Rost
serviert auf Zinnteller

Nürnberger Rostbratwürstl mit Weinkraut oder
Bamberger Meerrettich oder Kartoffelsalat

4 Stück	4,60
6 Stück	6,50
8 Stück	8,20

Die Speisekarte, bitte

When you ask for the menu in a restaurant you say **„Die Speisekarte, bitte"**. Often the menu is divided into sections, like those in the box below. Which name fits which drawing?

Can you complete the names of the five soups? An **Eintopf** is a thick vegetable soup, usually with meat or a sausage in it. It's a cross between a soup and a stew.

Learn these words before you go. They will help you understand the menu more quickly.

Die Speisekarte

Suppen	Vom Rind	Vom Huhn
		Fischgerichte
Eintopf	Vom Kalb	Pfannengerichte
Beilagen	Eierspeisen	Vom Schwein

Meine Lieblingsgerichte

*Hier sind meine Lieblingsgerichte!
Ich esse so gerne Schnitzel!*

A **Schnitzel** is a boneless piece of pork or veal (with a bone it's called a **Kotelett**). Sometimes we eat our **Schnitzel** with a hot sauce made of vegetables. For example, **Zigeunerschnitzel** has a tomato and green pepper sauce, **Jägerschnitzel** has a mushroom sauce. Sometimes we eat it on its own (**Natur-**). My real favourite is **Wiener Schnitzel**, which is coated in egg and breadcrumbs, and then fried. It is usually served **mit Zitrone, Pommes frites und Salat** – we often have a side salad instead of vegetables.

Which city do you think **Wiener Schnitzel** (in the photo on the right) gets its name from?

Ich heiße Günter. Ich trinke gern ein Bier zu meinem Schnitzel.

Another favourite of mine is **Schweinebraten** (on the left – roast pork), served here with **Salzkartoffeln, Erbsen, Möhren, Bohnen** and **Soße**.

Which of the following words fit other objects in the photo? **Gabel, Messer, Löffel, Untersatz, Gemüseschüssel, Teller, Tischdecke, Deckel, Weinglas.**

Herr Ober! Fräulein!

You say „**Herr Ober!**" or „**Fräulein!**" to call the waiter or waitress.

Using the **Speise-ABC** (page 50), work out what all the dishes on the menu above are. Which would you order? Work out what they would cost in pounds. Do you think this is expensive?

You say „**Zahlen, bitte**" when you want to pay the bill. Or you can ask for „**Die Rechnung, bitte**".

Usually **Bedienung** (service) and **Mehrwertsteuer** (VAT) are **inbegriffen** (included). You need to check on the menu whether the prices are **Inklusivpreise/Endpreise**, or whether service and VAT are extra.

If they want to leave a tip, Germans usually round up to the next mark or two.

With a partner, practise calling the waiter and ordering a meal (look at the menu above). Your partner must write down what you've ordered. Afterwards swap roles. Bob and his partner are already practising.

Übung macht den Meister

Fräulein! Ich möchte bestellen.

Bitte schön?

Einmal Jägerschnitzel mit Pommes frites und gemischtem Salat.

Jägerschnitzel ...

Buying a drink and a snack

What can you get at the snack bar?

Einen warmen Imbiß bekommst du am besten in einer Imbißstube.

- Most snack bars are counter-service, without a waiter or waitress.
- What does the word **Schnellimbiß** mean?
- Where do the motor-cyclists in the photo on the right come from? (Use the chart on pages 16-17.)

A snack bar in Freudenstadt, in the Black Forest.

This snack-van is on a motorway.

- You can buy a snack at vans like the one on the left. How much is potato salad?
- Which of the dishes below would you order?
- What if you were hungry and thirsty but only had 4 **DM** left?

Bechergetränke 0,25 1,50

Dosengetränke 1,80

Kaffee, Tee, Kakao 1,50

**Schnitzel 5,50
Jägerschnitzel 6,80
Zigeunerschnitzel 6,80**

Pommes frites 1,8

Currywurst 3,00

Bratwurst 2,70

Schaschlik 3,60

Reibekuchen mit Apfelmus 2,60

Frikadelle mit Brötchen 1,80

Möchtest du einen Hamburger?

Hamburgers are popular on the Continent too. Look at the ad on the right, outside a hamburger bar in Salzburg. What would you choose? And which currency are the prices in?

Just down the road, McDonald's has a special offer. Does it seem a good buy?

You'll notice ...

- that chips are served **mit Mayonnaise** or **mit Ketchup/Tunke** (tomato sauce), and with a little plastic fork.
- that tea is usually very weak, and is served in a glass either **mit Zitrone** (with lemon) or **mit Milch** (with milk).
- that coffee is served black with **Sahne** (cream) or with a little jug of **Kondensmilch** (unsweetened evaporated milk), and **Zucker** (sugar).

> **Eine Bratwurst und eine Cola, bitte.**

> **Bitte schön. Das macht 4,20 DM.**

Übung macht den Meister

With a partner, practise ordering dishes from these two pages. Your partner must tell you what the bill comes to.

Find out more

If you would like to know more about German food, send a stamped addressed envelope large enough for a booklet 26 cm × 19 cm to the German Food Centre, 44-46 Knightsbridge, London SW1X 7JN. They will send you their pamphlet *Food and Drink from Germany*. You can use this letter as a model:

Aberdeen, den 18. August

Sehr geehrte Damen oder Herren,
Ich bin Schülerin an einer Schule in Schottland, wo ich Deutsch lerne. Ich würde mich sehr darüber freuen, wenn Sie mir ein Exemplar Ihrer Broschüre "Food and Drink from Germany" zuschicken könnten.
Mit freundlichen Grüßen.
Kitty Strachan

Enjoy yourself!

Exploring the sights

It's fun exploring new towns and villages – they can be so different from our own. You might even explore a town in style, as here in Vienna in a horse-drawn **Fiaker**. What other horses is Vienna famous for?

The lazy way to explore!

Take it easy!

You can relax and learn at the same time by reading, watching television and listening to the radio. You won't understand much at first, but stick to it and see if you can get the gist.

Which of the magazines in the photo below, taken outside a kiosk in Salzburg, would you be tempted to buy?

An invitation

An invitation to a party. Can you go?

Einladung
Du bist herzlich eingeladen zu meiner Geburtstagsfête am 3. Juni um 8 Uhr

Edith

The drink in the big glass container is **Bowle**, punch. It is made of **Ananas** (pineapple), **Sekt** (German champagne) and **Weißwein** (white wine). **Köstlich!**

Übung macht den Meister

Gibt es hier in der Nähe ein Schwimmbad?

Find out what forms of entertainment there are in the area you visit. Like Bob, practise asking if there are the following:

- eine Diskothek
- ein Eisstadion
- ein Kino
- ein Theater
- ein Museum
- Tennisplätze

Sport rules everywhere

You'll find plenty of opportunity to get in on the action, because the Germans enjoy their sport to the full.

The lads in the photo have gathered in Leipzig in East Germany (along with another 25,000 young sportsmen and women) for the national **Spartakiade**, a big sports festival for young people. Each **Verein** (club) has its own distinctive colours, making the town a blaze of colour. Some of East Germany's most celebrated sports personalities have come to the forefront in this way, as the sign on the right, outside a sports shop, reminds us.

Peter Rost (**DDR**) plays handball, which is like a cross between basketball (the ball is passed from hand to hand) and football (you have to throw the ball past a goalkeeper into a small goal).

Maxi Gnauck (**DDR**) won three gold medals at her first **Spartakiade**.

Schöne Grüße aus Leipzig!

These English and German pupils have organised a **Tischtennisturnier** (table tennis tournament).

TOR! TOR!

Yes, it's a goal for Stuttgart in this **1. Bundesliga** (first division) match against Borussia Dortmund. This stadium in Dortmund was especially built for the 1974 **Fußballweltmeisterschaft** (World Cup championship).

The final score was 0-3.

Getting about by car

The journey across

> *Guten Tag! Ich bin es wieder. Willkommen in Deutschland! Hast du eine gute Fahrt gehabt?*

- What sort of journey did you have?
- How did you travel?
- How long did the journey take?
- Which countries did you travel through?
- Where did you enter Germany?
- How often did you have to show your passport?
- Draw a map like the one on page 14 and plot your route across, naming any major towns you passed.

> *Jetzt weiß ich endlich, daß ich Ferien habe!*

Holiday traffic jams are very common on motorways going South.

Schau dich um

- How many makes of petrol can you see?
- Which seems to be the most popular colour of car?
- Which seems to be the most popular make of car? Make a list like the one below, and put a tick every time you see one of these makes. After 15 minutes, count up. Who has won?

Beliebteste Automarken	
Opel	✓ ✓ ✓
Mercedes	✓ ✓
VW	✓ ✓ ✓
BMW	✓ ✓
Audi	✓ ✓
Ford	✓ ✓ ✓ ✓
ausländische Marken	✓

- Where do the cars come from (use the chart on pages 16-17)?
- Can you see any cars from abroad? If so, from which countries?

- Have you seen any Austrian vehicles? They have the first letter(s) of their **Bundesland** (see page 11). For example **W = Wien, St = Steiermark.** You may also see **G = Graz** and **L = Linz.**

S 233.926   **V 66.292**

A   **K 344·128**

T 51.343   **O.400.187**

Where do these Austrian cars come from?

At the service station

The motorway service station on the right is on one of the most beautiful of the West German motorways, between Aschaffenburg and Würzburg.

If you stop at such a service area, look and see which of these it has got: **ein Café** (a cafe); **ein Restaurant** (a restaurant); **Toiletten** (toilets); **ein Geschäft** (a shop); **Picknicktische** (picnic tables); **eine Tankstelle** (a petrol station); **ein Kinderspielplatz** (a playground). How would you compare it to any you've stopped at in Britain?

Can you see the **T** on the Steigerwald sign? What does it stand for?

Ich muß tanken!

Getting petrol

There are two grades of petrol in Germany, **Super** and **Normal**, but you can also get **Bleifrei** (leadfree). All petrol is sold in litres. There are about $4\frac{1}{2}$ litres in a gallon.

On the petrol pump, what does **Keine Selbstbedienung** mean? What does **Normal** cost?

The **Tankwart** (petrol pump attendant) is standing in front of some machines. What does **Erfrischungen** mean? What kind of **Erfrischungen** can you buy here?

Ich wünsche euch einen schönen Aufenthalt bei uns in Deutschland. Fahrt vorsichtig!

Distances in kilometres	Aachen	Basel	Berlin	Bonn	Karl-Marx-Stadt	Dortmund	Dresden	Frankfurt	Hamburg	Köln	Leipzig	München	Salzburg	Stuttgart	Wien
Aachen		566	633	91	593	150	659	259	488	70	585	648	788	446	907
Basel	566		874	482	721	571	787	337	820	496	720	362	488	268	765
Berlin	633	874		598	271	488	205	555	289	569	179	584	724	624	754
Bonn	91	482	598		509	120	575	175	459	27	501	364	704	362	828
Karl-Marx-Stadt	593	721	271	509		541	76	403	483	515	80	418	558	458	724
Dortmund	150	571	488	120	541		607	264	343	83	532	653	793	451	940
Dresden	659	787	205	575	76	607		469	502	589	108	484	624	524	799
Frankfurt	259	337	555	175	403	264	469		495	189	395	395	922	217	694
Hamburg	488	820	289	459	483	343	502	495		422	391	782	922	700	901
Köln	70	496	569	27	516	83	589	189	422		515	578	718	376	693
Leipzig	585	720	179	501	80	532	108	395	391	515		425	565	465	393
München	648	362	584	364	418	653	484	395	782	578	425		138	220	264
Salzburg	788	488	724	704	558	793	624	535	922	718	565	138		360	177
Stuttgart	446	268	624	362	458	451	524	217	700	376	465	220	360		414
Wien	907	765	754	828	724	940	799	694	901	693	393	264	177	414	

Übung macht den Meister

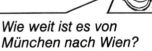

Wie weit ist es von München nach Wien?

Using the chart on the left, practise asking how far it is between any two towns. Also find out how far it is from where you are staying to the major towns in the area.

Settling in
Schau dich um

Look around at your accommodation.
- Is it attractively situated?
- What facilities does it offer?
- What signs and advertisements can you see? Are they like the ones on the hotels in Andernach (below)?

If you stayed in a hotel in Andernach, the Rhine valley would be on your doorstep. The photo below shows Katz Castle.

- How many people work there? What do they do? Are they all German?
- What nationality are the other guests?
- If it's a hotel, does it have any recommendations outside it, like the ones below, left? (What are the **ÖAMTC** and **ADAC** equivalents in Britain?)
- Does it have any specific rules and regulations?
- Has it got the price posted up in your room, as in the hotel below, right, in Freudenstadt?

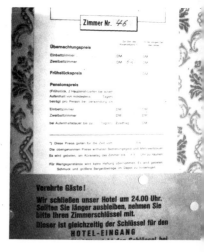

- What number is the room in the photo; and how many beds does it contain? What does it cost? What time does the hotel close; and what are you asked to do if you are going to be out after that time?
- Make a note of your room number and the name, address and telephone number of your accommodation. Don't forget to hang your key on the key-board when you go out!

Wo ist die Empfangsdame?

Was kannst du herausfinden?

Draw a map of the main streets near where you're staying and draw in any shops or other places you may need.

Ask where the following are:

> *Entschuldigen Sie, bitte. Wo ist hier in der Nähe ein Schreibwarengeschäft?*

Camping and Youth Hostelling

> *Ich hoffe, daß du nichts vergessen hast!*

1 Ich habe meinen Schlafsack mit.

2 Ich habe meine Luftmatratze . . .

3 . . . meinen Campingkocher.

4 Hier ist mein Geschirr

5 . . . und mein Besteck.

6 Ach, nein – ich habe mein Zelt vergessen!

We associate the River Ruhr with the industrial area of West Germany, but it's not all ugly. Here the Ruhr is passing a camp site at Hohensyburg.

CAMPING HOHENSYBURG

How much is the hostel?

How much would it cost you
- for a stay of three nights?
- to hire a sleeping bag
- to hire all your bed linen?
- for each meal?
- to have *all* your meals in the hostel?

Gebühren	
Übernachtungsgebühr für Junioren	6,—/6,50/7,— DM
Übernachtungsgebühr für Senioren	8,—/8,50/9,— DM
Leihgebühr für 1 Schlafsack (bis zu 10 Tagen)	1,70 DM
Leihgebühr für 2 Bettlaken (bis zu 10 Tagen)	2,— DM
für vollständige Bettwäsche bei Daueraufenthalten	
(1 Bettlaken, 1 Bettbezug, 1 Kopfkissen bis zu 10 Tagen)	3,— DM
Einzelmahlzeiten	ca. 3,— bis 6,— DM
Vollverpflegung	ca. 12,— bis 13,— DM

In a German home

Schau dich um

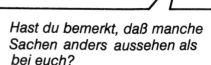

> Hast du bemerkt, daß manche Sachen anders aussehen als bei euch?

Look around any houses or flats you visit
- How many of the following are different: windows; letter-boxes; toilets; taps; electric plugs; light switches; curtains/shutters; beds; telephone?
- Have the windows got shutters?

With the handles horizontal, this type of door and window are wide open.

With the handles up, they open **auf Kipp** (leaning). With the handles down, they are **geschlossen** (shut).

- Do the windows and doors open like the ones above?
- Are all the electric plugs two-pin (with the earth on the edge of the rim)?
- Do flats have letter-boxes and a buzzer system like the one below? You ring the bell, and are asked through the loudspeaker who you are. You hear a buzzing noise, and you can push the door open.

Fernsterläden are shutters that open out.

Rolläden are shutters which wind down.

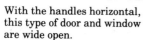

Was kannst du herausfinden?

Match the right name to each object. Then practise asking people if they have got the things at home.

> *Haben Sie einen Farbfernseher?*

eine Stereoanlage   eine Geschirrspülmaschine
eine Waschmaschine   ein Wäschetrockner
ein Videorekorder   ein Kassettenrekorder

Draw a plan of a house, labelling the rooms. Then make a list in German of everything in it.

Find out about the family!

1 „Was essen Sie am liebsten?"
„Mein Lieblingsgericht ist Gulasch mit Nudeln."

2 „Trinken Sie gern Wein?"
„O ja, vor allem Moselwein."

3 „Wie oft gehen Sie abends aus?"
„Nur selten. Wir sind immer zu müde."

4 „Fahren Sie oft in Urlaub?"
„Einmal im Jahr — meistens nach Spanien oder Italien."

5 „Was machen Sie am liebsten in Ihrer Freizeit?"
„Ich koche und backe gern und höre gern Musik."

6 „Was machen Sie nicht so gern?"
„So viele Fragen beantworten!"

Man muß die Feste feiern, wie sie fallen

Man muß die Feste feiern, wie sie fallen is a well-known German expression. What do you think it means? The Germans certainly love celebrating and they are good at it.

Ostersonntag
(Easter Sunday)

Children look in the garden for **Ostereier** (Easter eggs) and **Osterhasen** (Easter bunnies). Even normal eggs get painted and decorated.

◀ Their parents hid these children's eggs.

> *Ob ich das Parfüm bekommen habe, das ich mir gewünscht habe?*

Heiligabend
(Christmas Eve)

Most families don't put up their **Weihnachtsbaum** (Christmas tree) until December 24th. On the same day they have **Bescherung** (the opening of presents). Each member of the family has a **Weihnachtsteller** (a plate of nuts, fruit and chocolates). After dinner, which is traditionally **Gans** (goose) or **Karpfen** (carp), some people go to the midnight service at church.

Silvester (New Year's Eve)

At midnight **Sekt** is handed round. Then everyone goes out on to the street to welcome the new year with a fireworks display.

Frohes Neues Jahr!

Please write or phone

At the post office

Vergiß nicht, eine Ansichtskarte nach Hause zu schicken!

Have you noticed the sign below, left, outside any post offices? The other distinctive symbol for the German post is the horn which you can see on letter-boxes. All things postal – phones, letter-boxes, post buses and vans – are yellow.

POSTAMT

PAKETE	FERNGESPRÄCHE
POSTWERTZEICHEN	KLEINE MENGEN
EINSCHREIBEN	INLAND
EINZAHLUNGEN	

To buy stamps in the post office, look for the words **Briefmarken** or **Postwertzeichen** (stamps). To phone Britain, look for the sign **Ferngespräche** (long-distance phone calls). Look at the sign above, on the right. What can you do at this counter?

A post bus and, above, an old letter-box.

Ruf doch mal an

I'll surprise them back home and give them a ring!

What does the sign below, on the left, tell you about the calls you can make at this phone box?

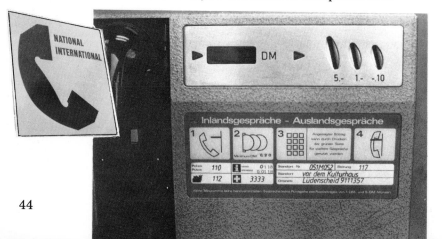

Here are the instructions in English, but put in the wrong order. Can you sort them out?

1 Dial the number
2 Unhook the receiver
3 Replace the receiver
4 Put in the money

In which town and in front of which building was this photo taken?

To ring Britain direct:
● Wait for the dialling tone
● Dial 0044 (Britain)
● Dial the code of your home town WITHOUT THE 0 at the beginning, for example London = 1, Edinburgh = 31
● Dial your own number!

Was kannst du herausfinden?

Und was kostet ein Brief nach Amerika, bitte?

You will need to know what it costs to send **ein Brief** (a letter) or **eine Postkarte** (a postcard) to Britain or to pen-friends in other countries. What is a **Briefwaage** (photo on the left)?

Look at the letter-box on the right and work out the time of the next collection, and the time of the collection on Saturday. The red dot above the times indicates a late collection, usually at about 11 p.m.

Don't forget the post code!

The two Germanies and Austria have a simple **Postleitzahl** (post code) system. As the map shows, the countries are divided into numbered regions. The major town in each region has this number as its code, for example **München** = 8. Other towns within this region then have two, three or four figure codes beginning with this number, for example **Nürnberg** = 85.

In Austria, **1 = Wien, 2 = Niederösterreich (Norden), 3 = Niederösterreich (Süden), 4 = Oberösterreich, 5 = Salzburgerland, 6 = Vorarlberg/Tirol, 7 = Burgenland, 8 = Steiermark, 9 = Kärnten.**

Which countries are these stamps from?

The **Briefträger** or **Postbote** (postman).

I'll show you round the town

Look at the map!

> We've popped across to East Berlin for the day. Let's not waste any time.

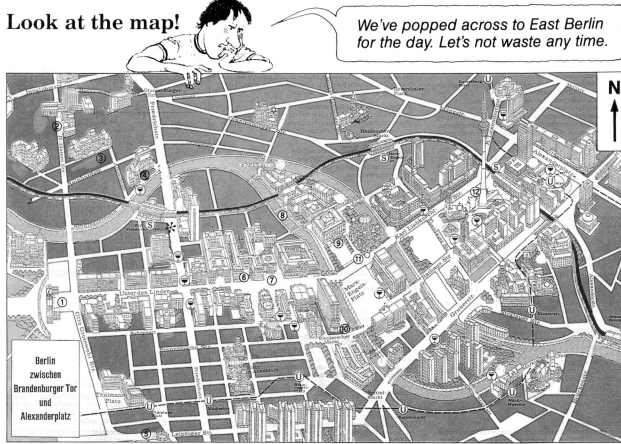

Berlin zwischen Brandenburger Tor und Alexanderplatz

You'll need to be able to ask the way to different places and to understand the answers. Practise with this map of East Berlin. You have just arrived at **Friedrichstraße** and are standing on the star ✳ facing south. Which of the sights above are these two people directing you to?

> *Du mußt zurückgehen, weiter die Friedrichstraße hinauf, über die Spree hinweg, und bieg sofort nach dem Brecht Theater links ein. Nimm die erste Straße rechts und du siehst das — direkt vor dir.*

> *Geh hier geradeaus und nimm die zweite Straße links. Geh geradeaus weiter an der Neuen Wache vorbei, und das — ist das große Gebäude direkt vor der Brücke auf der rechten Seite.*

Zur Orientierung
1 Brandenburger Tor 2 Akademie der Künste 3 Deutsches Theater 4 Brecht-Bühne 5 Postmuseum 6 Humboldt-Universität 7 Neue Wache 8 Pergamonmuseum 9 Altes Museum 10 Außenministerium 11 Berliner Dom 12 Fernsehturm

Übung macht den Meister

With a partner, practise giving instructions on how to get to some of the other sights of East Berlin.

> Ist es weit zum Fernsehturm?

> Ja, ziemlich. Geh . . .

Schau dich um

The **Osterstraße** in **Hameln**.

A café in the **Altstadt**, in Düsseldorf.

See what you can discover about any town you visit:

- How many inhabitants has it got?
- Was it badly destroyed in the War?
- Has it still got an **Altstadt** (old town), like this one in Düsseldorf (on the left)?
- What sort of public transport does it have?
- What entertainment does it provide for teenagers?
- Has it got any parks or nearby countryside?
- What industry is there in the area?
- Does it have a **Fußgängerzone** like the one above, in **Hameln**? (What is the English word for **Hameln**? And what is the story for which it is famous?)

Was bin ich von Beruf?

How many of the following have you seen working around the town? Can you put the missing words in their mouths? Make a note of all the jobs which you see people doing.

Müllmänner
Taxifahrerin
Pflastermaler
Straßenmusikanten
Lokführer
Polizist
Straßenverkäufer

> Ich bin — bei der Bundesbahn.

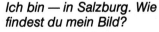

> Ich bin —.
> Ich lese Krimis, während ich warte.

> Wir sind — in Wien.

> Wir sind —.

> Ich bin — in Salzburg. Wie findest du mein Bild?

> Die Sachen sind so billig! Ich bin — in Köln.

> Ich bin — von Beruf.

Let's go shopping

Buying souvenirs and presents

What does **der kleine Laden** mean?

You'll notice that when German families are invited to eat at a friend's house, they usually take a present of flowers or chocolates. You will probably want to take home a few gifts. Go and buy them in a **Kaufhaus**, or at a souvenir stand.

No need to guess where the photo above, on the right, was taken! Buy postcards for your album as well as to send home.

One of the cheap and popular presents you can buy at the souvenir shop above, on the left, is **Aufkleber** (stickers). Look at the other ideas on this page.

Which are the most famous German makes of trainers and sports clothing? Work out your shoe size by adding 33 to your British size.

Take home some food that you've particularly enjoyed, like some of the many different types of sausage.

West Germany is famous for its attractive **Bierkrüge** (beer mugs). Work out what they cost in pounds.

What about some **Pralinen** (chocolates)? Lindt are a Swiss firm and their products are delicious.

Schau dich um

When you go shopping, look around.

- Can you see any major differences in the shops compared to those in Britain?
- How do prices compare? Which things seem cheaper than in Britain? Which seem more expensive?
- How do the prices of records, jeans, and books compare to those in Britain?
- What is the latest fashion in the boutiques?

A typical West German boutique.

n a big store, look for the sign **Kasse**. That's where you pay.

Übung macht den Meister

When you're out shopping, practise asking for prices, for example, **"Was kostet das T-Shirt, bitte?"**

Sonderpreis
CDs
29.00

T-Shirt
nur
12,50

Extra++ extra++ extra++

Kann ich diese Pullis anprobieren?

Der ist mir zu klein. Haben Sie den eine Nummer größer?

Der ist mir zu groß. Haben Sie den eine Nummer kleiner?

Der ist mir zu teuer. Haben Sie etwas Billigeres?

Die Farbe gefällt mir nicht. Haben Sie ihn in Rot?

Der gefällt mir sehr gut. Ich nehme ihn.

I know a good restaurant

Speise-ABC

Apfel – apple
Apfelmus – apple sauce
Apfelsine – orange
Aprikose – apricot
Banane – banana
Beilagen – extras (usually vegetables)
Bier – beer
Birne – pear
Blumenkohl – cauliflower
Bockwurst – type of sausage
Bohnen – beans
Braten – roast
Bratwurst – fried sausage
Champignons – mushrooms
Currywurst – fried sausage in hot sauce
Dosengetränke – canned drinks
Ei(er) – egg(s)
Eierspeisen – egg dishes
Eintopf – thick soup, stew
Eis – ice cream
Eisbein – pig's knuckle
Erbsen – peas
Erdbeeren – strawberries
Fanta – fizzy orange
Fisch(gerichte) – fish (dishes)
Fleisch – meat
Forelle – trout
Frikadelle – meat patty
Fruchtbecher – fruit with ice cream
Geflügel – poultry
gem(ischter) Salat – mixed salad
Gemüse – vegetables
Getränke – drinks
Gurke – cucumber
Hackfleisch – minced meat
Hähnchen – chicken
Himbeeren – raspberries
Honig – honey

Huhn – chicken
Jägerschnitzel – escalope in mushroom sauce
Johannisbeeren – red currants
Kakao – cocoa
Kalbfleisch – veal
Kartoffeln – potatoes
Kartoffelpüree – mashed potatoes
Kekse – biscuits
Kirschen – cherries
Klöße/Knödel – potato dumplings
koffeinhaltig – with caffeine
Kotelett – chop
Krabben – prawns
Kräuter – herbs
Kroketten – croquette potatoes
Lachs – salmon
Leber – liver
Limonade – fizzy drink
Linsen (suppe) – lentil (soup)
Masthähnchen – (fatted) chicken
Meerrettich – horseradish
Möhren – carrots
Niere(n) – kidney(s)
Nudel(n) – noodle(s)
Nuß – nut
Obst – fruit
Ochsenbraten – roast beef
Ochsenschwanz(suppe) – oxtail (soup)
Omelett – omelette
Orangensaft – orange juice
Pfannengerichte – fried dishes
Pfirsich – peach
Pilze – mushrooms
Pommes frites – chips
Pute – turkey
Reibekuchen – potato fritters
Reis – rice

Rindfleisch – beef
Rippen – spare ribs
Rosenkohl – Brussels sprouts
Rosinenstuten – currant bread
Rotkohl – red cabbage
Rühreier – scrambled eggs
Russisches Ei – egg mayonnaise
Saft – juice
Sahneschnitzel – escalope with cream
Salat – salad, lettuce
Salzkartoffeln – boiled potatoes
Sauerbraten – soured beef
Sauerkraut – pickled cabbage
Schaschlik – kebab
Schinken – ham
Schlag(sahne) – cream
Schnitzel – escalope
Schwarzbrot – black bread
Schweinefleisch – pork
Schweinshaxe – knuckle of pork
Senf – mustard
Soljanka – spicy meat and onion soup
Soße/Sauce – sauce, gravy
Spargel – asparagus
Spiegelei – fried egg
Suppe – soup
Tomate(n) – tomato(s)
Trauben – grapes
Waffeln – waffles
Wein – wine
Weinkraut – pickled cabbage
Weintrauben – grapes
Wiener Art – done in breadcrumbs
Wurst/Würstchen – sausage
Würzfleisch – seasoned meat
Zigeunerschnitzel – escalope with tomato and green pepper sauce
Zwiebeln – onions

Schau dich um

When you visit a restaurant, look around.
- What is the name of the restaurant?
- Is the menu divided into sections? If so, what do the sections mean?
- Are VAT and service included?
- Does the restaurant seem expensive to you?
- Is there a fixed-price menu?

If so, what does it cost? Is there much choice?
- What signs and adverts can you see around the restaurant?
- What are other customers eating and drinking?

Do remember ...

DO make a note of everything you try, and give it a mark out of three.

1 = **prima**   3 = **furchtba**

2 = **geht so**

Ich habe so einen Hunger

Zweimal Gulaschsuppe mit Brot, bitte.

Und zweimal Rumpsteak mit Pommes frites und Salat.

Und zwei Portionen Erbsen, bitte.

Und du? Hast du keinen Hunger?

Eating in East Germany

Mittagskarte von 11.30 bis 14 Uhr

Ukrainische Soljanka	1,85
Zitrone und Weißbrot	
Würzfleisch vom Geflügel	3,30
Zitrone, Weißbrot	
Ochsenbraten	3,80
in Rotweinsauce, frischer Salat, Kartoffelpürree	
Hühnerfrikassee	5,05
mit Kartoffelpürree, fr. Salat	
Klops mit Kapernsauce	4,—
frischer Salat, Kartoffelpürree	
Deutsches Beefsteak	3,65
Pommes frites, frischer Salat	
Ung. Gulasch	4,60
Kartoffelpürree, frischer Salat	
1/4 Broiler vom Grill	4,40
fr. Salat, Pommes frites	

East German restaurants are usually full, and you may well have to queue until a table is free. Every restaurant belongs to a fixed **Preisstufe** (price category). This menu is in **Preisstufe III**, the cheapest category. **Preisstufen II** and **I** restaurants are more comfortable and therefore more expensive. **Preisstufe S** (S=**Sonder**=Special) is the most luxurious.

What would you choose from the menu?

What other name is used for the dish which is called **Ochsenbraten** here?

What type of animal does the **Würzfleisch** (spiced meat) come from?

From which country does the **Gulasch** (goulash) originate?

Übung macht den Meister

With a partner, practise calling the waiter or waitress and ordering a meal from the menu on the left.

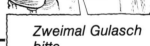

Zweimal Gulasch bitte.

DO collect beer mats, sugar packets, bills, colourful serviettes etc. for your album. The waiter or waitress may even let you have a menu.

1 Which countries do these three souvenirs come from?
2 Where is Stiegl beer brewed?
3 As well as being a restaurant, what is **MS Leipzig**?
4 Which town is the **Strandschlößchen** in?

A

B

C

Buying a drink and a snack

In the cafe

German cafes tend to be rather elegant and therefore quite expensive. You can sometimes get a hot snack in a cafe, but usually they sell only cake and ice cream to eat. They are often attached to a **Konditorei** (cake shop – photo above).

You can get alcoholic and non-alcoholic drinks in a cafe.

What would you order from the menu on the right?

What does the coke contain?

What juices can you order?

How do the prices compare to Britain?

The **Ku-damm (Kurfürstendamm)** in West Berlin, famous for its cafés, restaurants, shops and theatres.

These two girls have bought a **Stück Mohnkuchen** (piece of poppy seed cake).

Phantastisch!

Erfrischungsgetränke

240	Glas Coca-Cola *(koffeinhaltig)*	*0,2 l*	1.90
250	Glas Fanta	*0,2 l*	1.90
261	Flasche Reginaris		1.90
270	Glas Granini Apfelsaft	*0,2 l*	1.90
271	Glas Granini Orangensaft	*0,2 l*	2.50
212	Schorle weiß	*0,2 l*	2.50
213	Schorle rot	*0,2 l*	2.50
	Für den großen Durst:		
268	Limonade mit Zitronengeschmack	*0,2 l*	1.—
269	Limonade mit Zitronengeschmack	*0,4 l*	1.90

Warme Getränke

290	Tasse Kaffee		1.80
291	Portion Kaffee		3.60
292	Tasse Kaffee entkoffeiniert		1.80
293	Glas Tee mit Milch oder Zitrone		1.80
210	Glühwein	*0,2 l*	3.90
211	Grog von 4 cl echtem Übersee-Rum		4.—

- **Reginaris** is **Mineralwasser/Klarer Sprudel** (mineral water).
- **Schorle** is wine mixed with mineral water.
- A **Portion** or **Kännchen Kaffee** gives you two cups!
- **Glühwein** is a hot drink made of red wine, very warming in the winter.
- **Grog** is another hot alcoholic drink. What is it made of?

Übung macht den Meister

With a partner practise ordering a drink from the menu above.

Ich hätte gern ein Glas Tee mit Milch, bitte.

Zweimal Schokoladeneis, bitte

Das sieht gut aus!

PREISTAFEL
	DM
ab	-50
...el Eis	-25
...ion Sahne	-50
...becher	2,00
...chbecher	2,50
...eerbecher	2,60
...beerbecher	2,50
...asbecher	2,50
...eaubecher	3,50
...körbecher	3,00

These two boys have ordered **eine Portion Vanilleeis** (a vanilla ice). A **Becher** is a tub.

You can buy ice cream in cafes, at stands, and in ice cream parlours. What would you order from the stand in the photo? Which fruit flavours are mentioned? Which alcoholic flavours are on sale?

Judging by the prices, which country do you think the photo on the right was taken in?
Which of the ice creams looks the most tempting?
Which looks the most unusual?
What does **neu** mean?
Practise ordering your ice cream from this ad and from the stand on the left.

Spiel – – Spiel – – Spiel – – Spiel

Copy out these boxes, bigger, and then fill in the missing words (in German). The last letter of each word is the first letter of the next word. What is the vertical key word on the left?

1 fried sausage
2 plate
3 rice
4 soup
5 eggs
6 red cabbage
7 lentils
8 nut
9 steak
10 cocoa
11 omelette
12 tomatoes
13 noodle
14 salmon
15 juice
16 grapes
17 kidney
18 thick soup
19 fish
20 chicken

Schau dich um

Look around at snack bars, cafes and ice cream stands.
● What are most people drinking and eating?
● How do cafe prices compare with snack bar prices?
● Can you see any games and juke boxes?
● Are there any foreign ice cream parlours? If so, from which country?
● How many different types of sausage can you find (and eat!)? Make a note of everything you try and give it a mark out of three.

Where do these people come from?

What's different about school?

The school system

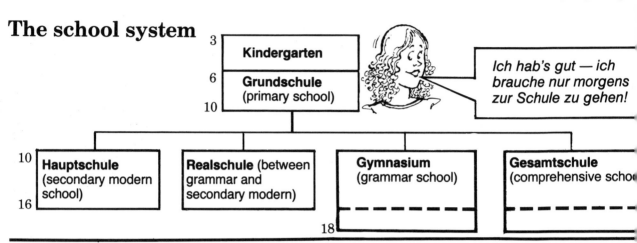

3	**Kindergarten**
6	**Grundschule** (primary school)
10	

Ich hab's gut — ich brauche nur morgens zur Schule zu gehen!

10	**Hauptschule** (secondary modern school)	**Realschule** (between grammar and secondary modern)	**Gymnasium** (grammar school)	**Gesamtschule** (comprehensive scho
16				
18				

Der Stundenplan

Look at the typical third-year (class 7) **Stundenplan** (timetable) on the right:

- What time does school start and end?
- Does the class have six lessons every day?
- What subjects have been abbreviated?
- How long does the class have between lessons?
- Is there a registration period?
- What religion is this pupil?

Stundenplan

Reiss für meine Augen — Blicki!

	Montag	Dienstag	Mittwoch	Donnerstag	Freitag	Samstag
8.00 – 8.45	Deutsch		Musik	Deutsch	Deutsch	Kunst
8.50 – 9.35	Englisch	Mathe	Mathe	Englisch	Sport	Chemie
9.55 – 10.40	Lat./Franz.	Geschichte	''	Chemie	Englisch	Musik
10.45 – 11.30	Erdkunde	Lat./Franz	Lat./Franz	Erdkunde	Lat./Franz	
11.45 – 12.30	Sport	Kath. Rel	Englisch	Kath Rel	Geschichte	
12.35 – 13.20	''		Deutsch	Kunst	Mathe	

Break

At break-time pupils go out in the **Schulhof** (playground). Some come to school by **Mofa**, a kind of small moped, which you can ride at the age of 15, although you need a special licence. Some older students at the school on the left come by **Motorrad** (motor bike). Nobody wears uniform.

Look at the chart on the left of the West German school system.

- At what age do pupils start primary school?
- At what age do they begin secondary school?
- At what age are they allowed to leave school?

The **Gesamtschulen** (comprehensive schools) are not as widespread as in Britain. Most **Länder** still prefer to split their pupils according to ability for their secondary education. What are the arguments for and against comprehensive schools?

Children don't start school until they are six, and even then they begin with a part-time timetable.

Most schools begin at about eight o'clock and end at lunchtime, though sometimes there are afternoon lessons for older pupils. There are lessons on Saturday morning too. Schools do not provide lunch. However, most comprehensives are **Ganztagsschulen** (all-day schools) and have a **Mensa** (canteen) where you can get lunch.

School pupils often carry a **Schultasche** (satchel).

Das Klassenbuch

> But how do they know who's absent if there's no registration?

Each class has a large book called a **Klassenbuch.** After every lesson the teacher enters in it what s/he has done with the class, and whether anyone was absent.

Read the extract from a **Klassenbuch** below. What subjects did the class have? And why was one pupil allowed to go home after period 4? In period 5 a **Klassenarbeit** (class test) was returned. These tests are usually marked on a 1-6 scale:

1 **sehr gut**
2 **gut**
3 **befriedigend**
4 **ausreichend**
5 **mangelhaft**
6 **ungenügend**

Your average **Note** (mark) in class tests, plus marks for giving answers in class, makes up the grade on your **Zeugnis** (report). If you get two fives or a six on your report, you will often have to **sitzenbleiben** (repeat a year).

Schau dich um

If you get a chance to visit a German school, look around:

- What are the buildings like?
- What are the pupils wearing?
- How do most come to school?
- What subjects do the pupils study?
- How many lessons do they have a day?
- How long are the lessons?
- What sorts of punishment are used?
- What sports do they do?
- Does the school have a **Raucherecke** (smokers' corner) in the playground for those over 16 who wish to smoke?

Extra++ extra++

To find out more about a school, ask a pupil these questions:
Was ist dein Lieblingsfach?
Was machst du in der Pause?
Was für eine Schule ist das?
Wieviele Schüler gehen zu deiner Schule?
Wieviele Hausaufgaben bekommst du?

Std	Fach	Aufgabe	Thema der Stunde	a) Versäumnisse b) Verspätungen	Bemerkungen	Namens-zeichen
	Erdk			**Montag**		
	Ma					
	Ku					
	Ku					
	Deu					
	Rel					

Von Montag, dem 7. 1.

55

What do the signs and ads mean?

Wo ist die Toilette?

Ich muß unbedingt zur Toilette.

It is important to understand the signs for toilets – it could save you a lot of problems!
Make sure you take some loose change along with you – there is often a charge.

Where was this photo taken?

How do you get to this toilet?

◀ Can you understand these two signs that you will find on the door?

▼ Here are five signs you may well see on or near other doors. What do they mean?

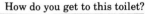

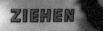

Following the signposts

This signpost is in Schiltach. What different sports can you do here? Do the people below need to go **rechts** or **links** at the signpost?

Wir wollen Tennis spielen

Ich möchte auf dem Markt etwas Obst kaufen.

Ich gehe schwimmen.

Ich gehe zum Turnverein.

Do the ads convince you?

> Die Reklamen bringen auf jeden Fall Farbe in die Stadt!

In West Germany you'll see a lot of colorful ads, like these two for Coca-Cola and oil.

In East Germany, most products are made by nationalized companies, so there is virtually no competitive advertising. Instead you see many political slogans and references to Karl Marx.

Look at the poster (above) being displayed in Meißen. What does it say about the purpose of Socialism?

Can you find out for what product Meißen is famous the world over?

Most factories in East Germany have slogans outside them referring to their production figures. Karl Marx died in 1883, so his portrait was particularly prominent in 1983.

Schau dich um

Make a note of signs you don't know. Also look at the advertisements.
- Where do you find advertisements?
- Which products are advertised most of all?
- What do the manufacturers claim about their products?
- Do cigarette advertisements carry a health warning?

Litfaßsäulen (advertising columns) used to be very common for advertising forthcoming events. Now some have been replaced by hoardings. What entertainments are advertised on this **Litfaßsäule?**

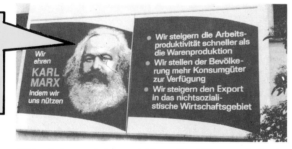

> Bin ich schon 100 Jahre tot? Meine Güte, wie die Zeit verfliegt!

This photo was taken outside an East German factory.

Any advertising there is in East Germany is often seen on bridges.

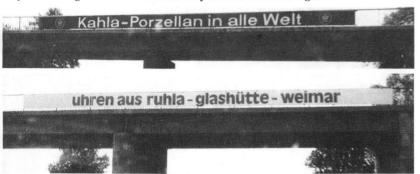

57

HELP!

At the doctor's

Vergiß nicht dein Versicherungsformular, wenn du bei uns zum Arzt gehst.

There is no national health service in West Germany, so if you have to visit a doctor, take your E111 form or any other insurance form you have. The sign outside the doctor's tells you the times of the **Sprechstunden** (surgery).

univ. med.
Dr. Bernhard Lang
Prakt. Arzt
Ordination: 8 – 11 Uhr
außer Donnerstag
Eingang rückwärts

Dr. med. **M. Witte**
prakt. Arzt

Sprechstunden
Mo – Fr 8 – 11
Di u. Fr 16 – 18

How many morning surgeries are there a week? On which afternoons can you see the doctor?

„Eingang rückwärts". Does that mean I have to walk in backwards?

One of the doctor's nameplates above is Austrian, the other is German. The doctor's title is expressed differently, and there are two more differences:

Austrian	*German*
Ordination	**Sprechstunden**
rückwärts	**hinten**

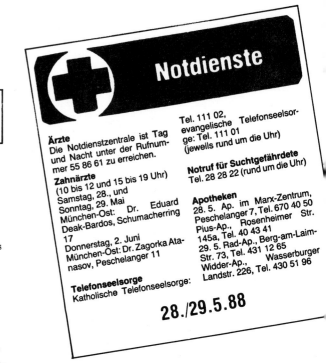

Notdienste

Ärzte
Die Notdienstzentrale ist Tag und Nacht unter der Rufnummer 55 86 61 zu erreichen.

Zahnärzte
(10 bis 12 und 15 bis 19 Uhr)
Samstag, 28., und Sonntag, 29. Mai
München-Ost: Dr. Eduard Deak-Bardos, Schumacherring 17
Donnerstag, 2. Juni
München-Ost: Dr. Zagorka Atanasov, Peschelanger 11

Telefonseelsorge
Katholische Telefonseelsorge:

Tel. 111 02, evangelische Telefonseelsorge: Tel. 111 01 (jeweils rund um die Uhr)

Notruf für Suchtgefährdete
Tel. 28 28 22 (rund um die Uhr)

Apotheken
28. 5. Ap. im Marx-Zentrum, Peschelanger 7, Tel. 670 40 50
Pius-Ap., Rosenheimer Str. 145a, Tel. 40 43 41
29. 5. Rad-Ap., Berg-am-Laim-Str. 73, Tel. 431 12 65
Widder-Ap., Wasserburger Landstr. 226, Tel. 430 51 96

28./29.5.88

If it's out of surgery hours, consult the local newspaper to see which doctor is on emergency call.

The extract above, from a Munich paper, gives the emergency numbers for a weekend in May. Which number should you ring to find out which emergency doctor is on duty? And if you need to ring a chemist on Saturday?

What is the **Telefonseelsorge**? And what are **Suchtgefährdete**?

Was ist los?

Ich habe solche Halsschmerzen.

Und ich habe Magenschmerzen.

*Und ich habe Fieber.
Und ich habe Kopfschmerzen.*

Und ich bin so erkältet.

Sonst geht 's mir gut!

At the chemist's

If you get a **Rezept** (prescription) from a doctor, take it to the **Apotheke**. If the chemist's is shut, the sign outside will tell you which one is on emergency standby. What are **Rezepteinwurf** and **Nachtglocke**?

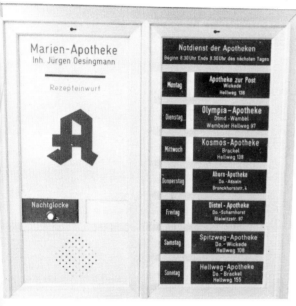

At the **Apotheke** you can ask for advice about minor ailments.

Ich habe mein Herz in Heidelberg verloren!

This is the first line of a popular old German song. What does it mean?

If you've lost anything else of value, go to the **Polizeiwache** (police station) or **Fundbüro** (lost property office).

If you lose your passport, you'll need to be able to say „**Entschuldigen Sie, bitte. Ich habe meinen Paß verloren!**" Practise saying that you have lost the six things below.

What have these three left behind?

1 Entschuldigen Sie, bitte. Habe ich meinen Regenschirm hier liegenlassen?

2 Entschuldigung! Habe ich meine Brieftasche hier liegenlassen?

3 Entschuldigen Sie! Habe ich meine Handschuhe hier liegenlassen?

Übung macht den Meister

Practise asking for something for different aches and pains. (How do we know Bob is in the South?).

Grüß Gott. Haben Sie etwas gegen Durchfall und Grippe?

Pinimenthol-S

Für Säuglinge und Kleinkinder

Zusammensetzung:
Ol. Eucal. 10,8 g, Ol. Pini silv. 10,8 g, Ol. Pini Pumil. 1,4 g, Ol. Terebinth. 2,0 g, Salbengrundlage ad 100,0 g.

Gebrauchsanweisung:
Erbs- bis haselnußgroßes Stück Salbe 2-4 mal täglich auf Brust und Rücken einreiben bzw. zum Inhalieren in ein Gefäß mit heißem Wasser geben.

Zum Einreiben oder Inhalieren

Dosierungsanleitung

Soweit nicht anders verordnet, Erwachsene und Jugendliche: 1mal täglich 1/2–1 Teelöffel, Kinder ab 6. Lebensjahr, je nach Alter: 1mal täglich 1/4–1/2 Teelöffel Liquidepur am besten abends einnehmen.

Vor Gebrauch schütteln!
Wirkungseintritt nach 8–10 Stunden.
Das Arzneimittel soll nach Ablauf des Verfalldatums nicht mehr angewandt werden.

Arzneimittel unzugänglich für Kinder aufbewahren!

Make sure you can understand the instructions on medicines:
1 In which two ways can the **Salbe** (ointment) be used?
2 How many teaspoons should you take of the medicine? How often? When is the best time to take it?

Who's in the news?

Reading the newspaper

(A) **London: Große Mehrheit gegen die Todesstrafe**

(B) **Bombe am Kurfürstendamm Ein Toter und 23 Verletzte**

(E) **Noch einmal singen die „Beatles" – für den Prince of Wales**

(D) **Ed Moses: Nun 107 Mal ungeschlagen**

(F) **Zum Mai-Ende Schneetreiben auf der Zugspitze**

(C) **Die US-Girls stehen auf Europe**

(G) **Noch 50 000 Jugendliche sind ohne Lehrstelle**

(H) **Landung auf dem Roten Platz**

Peter Groß, West Germany's most famous swimmer.

The world-famous Austrian conductor, Herbert von Karajan.
Top right: **Bundeskanzler** (Chancellor) Kohl, elected in 1983.

Look at German newspapers and magazines. Which famous people are in the headlines and why? Make a note of headlines you can understand, as well as new words and phrases you have learned from the newspapers and magazines.

Look at the headlines (above) from West German newspapers and answer these questions.

1 What was the weather like on the **Zugspitze** at the end of May?
2 What is special about the concert attended by the Prince of Wales?
3 What do American girls think about the pop group 'Europe'?
4 Where did a young West German pilot land?
5 How many casualties were caused by a bomb in Berlin?
6 What happened to Ed Moses 107 times?
7 What are 50,000 young people still without?
8 What vote was taken in London, and with what result?

1 La Isla bonita (2) 7. Wo. **Madonna**		**19** Heat of the Night (29) 3. Wo. **Bryan Adams**	
2 Face your Life (3) 5. Wo. **Pierre Cosso**		**20** I come undone (12) 8. Wo. **Jennifer Rush**	
3 Don't break my Heart (7) 5. Wo. **Don Harrow**		**21** Livin' on a Prayer (21) 20. Wo. **Bon Jovi**	
4 You're the Voice (4) 9. Wo. **John Farnham**		**22** Meet el Presidente **Duran Duran**	
5 Respectable (5) 8. Wo. **Mel & Kim**		**23** Down to Earth (24) 2. Wo. **Curiosity killed the Cat**	
6 Stay (1) 11. Wo. **B. Blanco & Pierre Cosso**		**24** Heartbeat (27) 25. Wo. **Don Johnson**	
7 Let it be (9) 4. Wo. **Ferry Aid**		**25** Skin Trade (19) 14. Wo. **Duran Duran**	
8 Nothing's gonna stop us now (6) 5. Wo. **Starship**			
9 Stand by me (10) 9. Wo. **Ben E. King**			
10 With or without you (13) 4. Wo. **U 2**			
11 Manhattan Skyline (8) 11. Wo. **a-ha**			
12 Strangelove (26) 4. Wo. **Depeche Mode**			
13 Live it up **Mental as Anything**		**26** Voice on a Hotline **Don Johnson**	
14 Miss you so **Connie Blanco**		**27** Engel der Nacht (22) 13. Wo. **Nena**	
15 I just can't wait (15) 7. Wo. **Mandy**		**28** Heartache (16) 12. Wo. **Pepsi & Shirlie**	
16 Carrie (11) 14. Wo. **Europe**		**29** Ich liebe dich (17) 18. Wo. **Clowns & Helden**	
17 Dominoes (18) 5. Wo. **Robbie Nevil**		**30** Everything I own (20) 5. Wo. **Boy George**	
18 Heartache away (14) 11. Wo. **Don Johnson**			

ook at the charts above. These records were its during a week in June 1987. How many of he songs do you know?

Who's in the hit-parade?

Have a look in one of the teenage magazines like **Bravo** for this week's hit-parade.

● How many of the songs are sung in German?
● How many are sung by German singers or groups?
● How many are British or American?
● What's your favourite in the charts?

A famous Austrian singer, Falco.

Who's top of the Bundesliga?

One of Germany's greatest stars is orward Karl-Heinz Rummenigge. He sed to be captain of West Germany.

There are two national football leagues in West Germany, the
1. Bundesliga and the
2. Bundesliga. All other football is played at regional level. Why do you think this is?

Here is the **Tabelle** (league table) after 31 games.

● Look at the list of cities on page 20. Which is the largest city without a first division team?
● What do the column headings stand for?
● What do you think **FC** means?
● The **B.** in front of **München** tells you which **Land** this team is from. What is it?

The **Tabelle** tells you how many points each team has dropped as well as gained. For example, **FC Schalke 04** have gained 29 points and have dropped 33 points. How many points are given for a win?

Karl-Heinz Rummenigge (on the right in the photo) has a brother who plays for **Bayern München.** He is also a **Nationalmannschaft** (national team) member. Can you find out his name? Where's his team in the **Tabelle**?

Tabellenstand

	Sp.	g.	u.	v.	Tore	Diff.	Pkt.
1. (1.) B. München (M, P)	31	18	12	1	61:28	+33	48-14
2. (2.) Hamburger SV*	31	17	8	6	60:33	+27	42-20
3. (5.) Bor. M'gladbach*	31	15	7	9	62:41	+21	37-25
4. (3.) Borussia Dortmund	31	13	10	8	63:43	+20	36-26
5. (4.) Werder Bremen*	31	15	6	10	57:51	+6	36-26
6. (8.) Kaiserslautern*	31	14	7	10	58:44	+14	35-27
7. (7.) 1. FC Köln	31	13	9	9	46:42	+4	35-27
8. (6.) Bayer Leverkusen*	31	14	6	11	47:34	+13	34-28
9. (9.) VfB Stuttgart	31	13	6	12	52:39	+13	32-30
10. (10.) 1. FC Nürnberg*	31	11	9	11	45:44	+1	31-31
11. (11.) Bayer Uerdingen*	31	9	12	10	47:38	+9	30-32
12. (12.) VfL Bochum*	31	11	7	13	46:55	−9	29-33
13. (13.) FC Schalke 04	31	10	8	13	48:62	−14	28-34
14. (14.) Waldhof Mannheim	31	7	9	15	38:45	−7	23-39
15. (15.) Eintracht Frankfurt*	31	5	8	18	27:72	−45	18-44
16. (17.) FC Homburg (N)*	31	6	5	20	37:84	−47	17-45
17. (16.) Fortuna Düsseldorf	31	2	11	18	29:71	−42	15-47
18. (18.) BW 90 Berlin (N)							

DDR-Oberliga	Gesamt	
	Tore	Punkte
1. Dynamo Berlin	72:22	46-6
2. FCV Frankfurt/O	56:29	34-18
3. FC Jena	46:29	34-18
4. FC Lok Leipzig	45:27	31-21
5. Rot-Weiß Erfurt	45:37	31-21
6. 1. FC Magdeburg	52:32	29-23
7. Dynamo Dresden	51:43	29-23
8. Hansa Rostock	38:40	28-24
9. Karl-Marx-Stadt	41:41	26-26
10. Wismut Aue	30:45	20-32
11. Chemie Halle	41:53	17-35
12. Union Berlin	23:50	17-35

The top of the **Oberliga**, the East German equivalent of the **Bundesliga.** The East German and Austrian teams have not been as successful as the West Germans, but football is still popular in both countries.

Enjoy yourself

Macht's dir Spaß?

Talk to as many people as possible, visit new places and do different things. For example, if you get the opportunity, look around a German factory or works.

This group of pupils from Britain are being shown around an electrical power station in Werne. It provides most of the electricity for the **Ruhrgebiet**.

The **Volksprater Vergnügungspark**, a big and famous fun fair in Vienna.

Was kannst du herausfinden?

1 lesen
2 Freunde treffen
3 schwimmen
4 Musik hören
5 Fußball spielen
6 faulenzen
7 radfahren
8 Tennis spielen
9 Handarbeiten
10 reiten

Find out from young people what they most enjoy doing in their spare time. Make a "top ten" of the most popular activities, and compare it with the one on the left. This one was compiled by asking 14-year-old pupils, in various schools in West Germany and Austria, what they do in their spare time: **Was machst du am liebsten in deiner Freizeit?** See if you get any answers like the ones in these drawings.

Ich reite sehr gern!

Ich boxe gern — aber nicht besonders gut.

Ich faulenze gern. Ich brauche mir keine Sorgen zu machen.

Ich sehe den ganzen Tag fern.

Ich fahre jeden Winter ski.

Was kommt heute im Fernsehen?

There are three channels on West German television, though the **3. Programm** is different in the North from the South. Some Germans now have cable television, which offers up to 15 channels, including three in English and two in French.

Look at the extract:

- Can you find out what day of the week these programmes are on?
- What is the programme that starts at 12.45 pm on the first channel about?
- How many films can you watch?
- Which countries are these films from?
- What does **ZDF** stand for?
- What time does the cartoon start?
- What is the news programme on the second channel called?
- What is the film that starts at 2.40 pm on the second channel about?

On German television, films and news are not interrupted by advertisements. There are special times for advertisements, usually before the evening programmes start.

East Germany has two television channels, and so has Austria, but people in both countries often tune in to West German television as well.

Schau dich um

- What entertainment is there for young people in the area where you are staying?
- Do the teenagers visit each other's homes a lot?
- Do they do a lot of sport or active exercise?
- Do they spend a lot of time watching television? How do programmes compare with Britain?
- Look at the daily paper or one of the television/radio magazines like **Hör zu**, find out what's on television, and how many programmes are American or British.

Was läuft im Kino?

Auch in Dortmund gibt es viele Kinos. Letzte Woche habe ich Over the top *gesehen — super.*

Take a look at a local paper or look at theatre listings.
Here is an extract from a major newspaper in Munich. Do you recognise any of the films?

- What time is the first showing of *Over the top*?
- Who do you think goes to **Kinderkino**?
- How long has *Asterix* been on in Munich?
- How old have you got to be if you want to see *Platoon*?
- What day is *Tod in Venedig* shown on?

The West German film industry has been very successful internationally in recent years. Films by directors such as Wim Wenders, the late Rainer Maria Fassbinder and Werner Herzog are often shown on British television.

Did you like the food?

Rückblick

- Which meals and drinks did you most enjoy?
- Which did you least enjoy?
- Which were the most different from anything you've eaten at home?

- What nationalities of restaurant did you see?
- Which countries are represented below? (Find another on page 74.)

- Did you see people having a barbecue? **Grillen** is very popular in the summer – some butchers even sell specially spiced meat.

Traudi and Helmut are barbecuing **Rippen** (spare ribs).

Bei diesem schönen Wetter esse ich lieber im Garten!

Did you get invited to anyone's house or go into a cafe for **Kaffee und Kuchen** (coffee and cakes)? This is a popular custom, particularly on Saturday or Sunday afternoon, at about four o'clock. The **Kaffee** is made from freshly-ground beans, and the **Torte** (flan) or **Kuchen** are eaten with **Schlagsahne** (whipped cream).

Can you remember the names?
In the **Bergisches Land** near **Düsseldorf** they offer bread, jam and **Quark** (curd cheese) as well as coffee and cake. Can you label the things in the photo on the right with these words:

Johannisbeerkuchen	Honig
Butter	Quark
Kondensmilch	Schwarzbrot
Zucker	Rosinenstuten
Marmelade	Kaffee

Apfelstrudel

250g Mehl, 1 Ei, eine Priese Salz, Oel, ⅛l warmes Wasser. Das Ganze gut kneten u. 20 Min. unter einer warmen Schüssel rasten lassen. Ausziehen, mit zerlassener Butter beträufeln u. mit blätterig gesch. Äpfeln, Rosinen, Zucker, Zimt u. in Butter angerösteten Bröseln bestreuen, zusammenrollen, auf ein befettetes Backblech legen u. bei Mittelhitze eine ½ Std. goldgelb backen.

> *Schau mal — es ist so leicht einen Apfelstrudel zu backen.*

A taste of Austria

You may have tried **Apfelstrudel** (apple pastry) whilst you were abroad. It's not difficult to make and it tastes delicious. Try making it from the recipe on this Austrian dishcloth.

In the photo on the right, Marianne (who lives in Salzburg) has stretched the **Apfelstrudel** dough out over the table and has covered it with the filling. She is now turning in the sides, so that the filling doesn't fall out. Next she will make the strudel into a long roll, and will put it in the oven.

> *Hast du die Schilder alle verstanden?*

Did you see any signs like the ones above? What do they mean? And what is the German word for what the Austrians call **Schlag**?

Travelling around

Rückblick

- How many forms of transport did you use?
- Did you find public transport efficient? Cheap?
- What did you think of German drivers? How do they compare to the British in terms of speed and care?
- Were you near a town with a **U-bahn** (underground)? Munich had its underground specially built for the 1972 Olympics. Much older is the one in Berlin (photo on the right).

- Did you see:
- A lorry with a long trailer? Trailers and caravans have different number plates from the vehicle pulling them, because they are registered separately.
- A luxury tourist coach? They have **Video, Stereoanlage, Toilette, Bar, Klimaanlage** (air conditioning) and **Luftfederung** (air suspension).
- People going to school by **Schulbus** (school bus, photo on the right)?

Vorsicht!

Jedes Glas ist zuviel

There are determined efforts throughout German-speaking Europe to cut down the number of accidents on the roads. What do the two signs in East Germany (below and left) mean? And the message in West Germany?

In the mountains, **Schneeketten** (snow chains) are an important part of a driver's equipment. Why are they used? What sort of car is the one on the far right?

Was hast du sonst für Schilder gesehen?

You may have seen a sign for **Frankfurt a. M. Frankfurt am Main** is in West Germany, on the River Main; **Frankfurt an der Oder** is in East Germany, on the Oder.

The East Germans never refer to East Berlin, they only talk of **Berlin, Hauptstadt der DDR,** and **Westberlin.**

Which of these signs means Motorway exit? Diversion? Motorway merger? Accident?

Anagrams – – Anagrams – –

Look at these West German number plates. Which towns do the cars come from?

Can you form a German word out of the letters of each number plate and link it up to one of the definitions on the right?

1 eine Blume
2 etwas im Gesicht
3 ein Tier
4 etwas am Himmel
5 ein Behälter
6 jemand aus Großbritannien
7 etwas zu essen
8 wie man heißt
9 eine westdeutsche Stadt
10 Kurzform von 'Johannes'

OS DE 975

M·UL 4710   EN-AS 750   SO·RE 793

EBE-RL 51   DO-NM 487   BIT·RE 56

NE-MA 63   HN·AS 433   ES·HA 3199

Ein deutscher Witz!

Wie heißt der chinesische Transportminister?

Um – lei – tung

If you break down, the **ADAC (Allgemeiner Deutscher Automobil-Club)** will help. If you belong to an affiliated organisation, such as the AA, and have a **Schutzbrief** (5-star insurance), there is no charge.

When you drive in West Germany you must have your **Führerschein** (driving licence), **Kraftfahrzeugschein** (car registration document), **Erste Hilfe** (first aid box) and a **Warndreieck** (warning triangle).

Each car must regularly undergo a **TÜV (Technischer Überwachungsverein)** a mechanical check, and an **ASU (Abgassonder-untersuchung),** exhaust emission check.

Was school different?

Rückblick

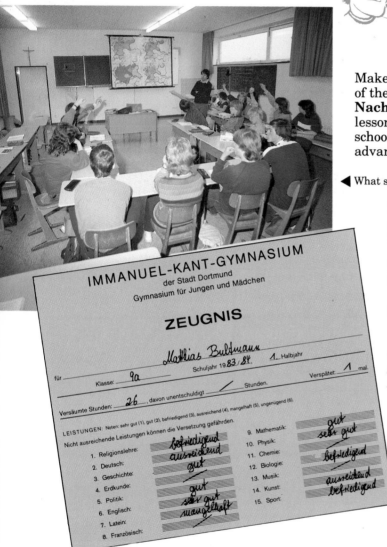

> I found out that the equivalent of our first form is **Klasse 5** (following on from four years of primary school).

Make two lists, one of the **Vorteile** (advantages) of the German school system, and one of the **Nachteile** (disadvantages). If you sat in on any lessons, how did the behaviour compare to your school in Britain? Did the work seem very advanced? Were the teachers strict?

◄ What subject is probably being taught in this lesson?

Did you see a school report? Pupils receive one at the end of each **Halbjahr** (term). There are only two terms in Germany.

Look at Matthias Bultmann's report. How many times has he been late in this half year?

Which are his best subjects? And which subject did he fail in?

Do you think he will have to **sitzenbleiben**

Did you see any pupils starting school? On their very first school day, at the age of six, they receive a **Schultüte** full of sweets and chocolates.

IMMANUEL-KANT-GYMNASIUM
der Stadt Dortmund
Gymnasium für Jungen und Mädchen

ZEUGNIS

Matthias Bultmann

für _____ Klasse: 9a _____ Schuljahr 19 83 / 84. 1. Halbjahr _____ Verspätet: 1 mal.

Versäumte Stunden: 26, davon unentschuldigt / Stunden.

LEISTUNGEN: Noten: sehr gut (1), gut (2), befriedigend (3), ausreichend (4), mangelhaft (5), ungenügend (6).
Nicht ausreichende Leistungen können die Versetzung gefährden.

1. Religionslehre: befriedigend	9. Mathematik: gut
2. Deutsch: ausreichend	10. Physik: sehr gut
3. Geschichte: gut	11. Chemie: befriedigend
4. Erdkunde:	12. Biologie:
5. Politik: gut	13. Musik: ausreichend
6. Englisch: sehr gut	14. Kunst: befriedigend
7. Latein: mangelhaft	15. Sport:
8. Französisch:	

East German children with their **Schultüte**.

Anagrams – – Anagrams – –

Unjumble the names of the s objects in the drawing.

THEF   MURDERMAGII
CHUB   LUKI
NELLIA   FISTIBELT

Can you unjumble these school subjects?

SCHINGLE   PROST
STUNK   GICHECHEST
PSYKHI   MAKETIMHAT
CHUSTED   BIGLOOIE
MICHEE   DEERDUNK

Wandertag

> *Ab und zu haben wir einen Wandertag, wo die Klasse irgendetwas unternimmt.*

> *Diese Wandertage sind fas so anstrengend wie die Schule!*

The class above are listening to a talk by a **Förster** (ranger), about the upkeep of German forests. The boy on the left has found a new **Raucherecke**...

At least once a year each class has a **Wandertag** (hiking day). They go off with their **Klassenlehrer(in)** (class teacher) for a long walk in the country, or sometimes to a zoo or other form of entertainment. The class usually has lunch in the open air.

Did you know?

The German equivalent of A-levels is the **Abitur** (in Austria it's called the **Matura**), which encompasses a number of subjects. The average mark of all your **Noten** on your **Abiturzeugnis** decides whether you can go on to further study.

There is no real equivalent of O-levels. If you leave school at 15 or 16, you receive an **Abschlußzeugnis** (leaving report), with your grade for that year on it.

Many children of **Gastarbeiter** (foreign workers) attend German schools. What special problems do you think these pupils may have?

In East Germany pupils of 6 to 16 attend a **polytechnische Schule** (comprehensive school where technical and scientific subjects are emphasised). At the age of 10 they start their first foreign language, which is Russian. From the age of 13, a whole or half day a week is spent on a farm or in a factory. There are also specialist schools for pupils with a particular talent in some subject or sport.

This chart shows the number of foreign pupils in West German schools. What nationality are the majority? Below: a lesson in a **polytechnische Schule.**

Junge Ausländer an deutschen Schulen

An den allgemeinbildenden Schulen der Bundesrepublik Deutschland sind insgesamt **695 700** ausländische Schüler.
davon:

Nationalität	Prozent
Türken	51,5 %
Italiener	11,5 %
Jugoslawen	10,4 %
Griechen	7,5 %
Spanier	3,5 %
Portugiesen	2,7 %
Sonstige	12,9 %

What did you buy?

Rückblick

What did you buy, for yourself or as presents, while you were away? Did you find things expensive? What would you recommend other visitors to Germany to buy?

Im Sonderangebot

Did you see many things **im Sonderangebot** (on special offer)? Were you there during the sales, for example the **Sommerschlußverkauf** or **SSV** (summer sales)?

Special offers are often advertised in shop windows, as in the supermarket in Munich on the right. Look at the photo:
- What are the twelve things on special offer?
- Which of them could you buy in a British supermarket?
- How do the prices compare?

Look at the ad (below) for the **SSV** at Karstadt, one of the biggest stores:
- What time does the store open?
- How long does the sale last?
- How can you tell which things are on special offer when you are in the shop?
- What material are the handbags made of?
- How much do fashionable dresses cost?
- How much are the men's pyjamas?
- What can you get for 1 **DM**? And for 3 **DM**?

Could you follow the signs?

Which of these signs would you follow if you wanted to buy the things on this shopping list?

Einkaufsliste

1 kg. Apfelsinen
Blumenkohl
100 gr Salami
Glas Kaffee
Knoblauch & Pfefferkörner
2 kiwis
4 gefr. Schnitzel
Portemonnaie
After-shave
Zündkerzen

GEWÜRZE aktuell + preiswert!

frisches Gemüse

LEDERWAREN

frisches Obst

AUTOZUBEHÖR

Look at these symbols ▶ outside a sports shop. Which of the following sports goes with which symbol?

Tennis
Skilaufen
Judo
Schlittschuhlaufen
Tischtennis
Fußball
Volleyball

Collecting wrappers

Did you collect wrappers and labels to stick in your album?

These labels and wrappers are from West German, East German and Austrian products.

● From which animal is the liver sausage?

● How much do the peanuts cost, and for what quantity?

● From which fish is the **Salat** made?

The Germans eat a lot of different salads when they have a cold evening meal or a barbecue. For example, **Thunfischsalat** (tuna-fish salad), **Kartoffelsalat** (potato salad), **Eiersalat** (egg salad).

71

Did you enjoy yourself?

Was war der Höhepunkt deines Aufenthalts?

Rückblick

When you think back over your stay:
- What were the highlights?
- Were there any bad moments?
- Did you meet many people?
- Did you go to any parties or discos?
- Did you do anything new, like **kegeln** (indoor bowling)? **Kegelbahnen** (bowling alleys have only nine pins, and the bowl is smaller than for ten-pin bowling. Often a whole neighbourhood or firm goes bowling together.
- Did you go up a mountain in a **Seilbahn** (cable car) or **Skilift** – or the hard way: on foot?

Dancing – mostly to English music – in a West German disco. On the right: This cable car takes you to the top of the **Pfänder** mountain in Bregenz, on the **Bodensee**. What do we call the **Bodensee**?

This group of Austrians have just walked up the **Untersberg** outside Salzburg. They took two hours.

- Did you go to a **Kirmes** (fair) or to any theme parks in Germany? One of the biggest is **Phantasialand** in Brühl, west of Cologne. There are **Achterbahnen** (big dippers), a **Wildweststadt** (frontier town) and a recreation of **Altberlin** (old Berlin).

Enjoying the water

Germany has little coastline but there are a lot of lakes where people sun-bathe, swim, go wind surfing etc.

A fountain in Leipzig on a hot summer's day. On the right: **Windsurfen** on the **Fuschlsee** in the **Salzkammergut**. Which country is it in?

Es ist nicht so leicht wie es aussieht!

War es teuer?

Did you find it expensive over there? What were entrance prices like, for example?

The usual price for a ticket for the cinema below is between 7 and 9 **DM**. When can you get in for 6 **DM**?

How much does it cost to hire roller skates here?

What would it cost ▶ you to get into this zoo? And how much for permission to use a camera? How do you know the zoo is in East Germany?

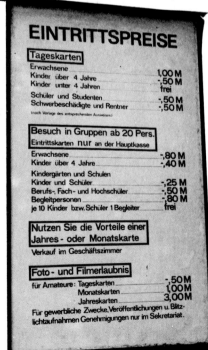

73

So many signs and ads!

Glamour signs

I saw some beautiful signs outside shops and hotels. You should see the Macdonald's sign in Salzburg!

A

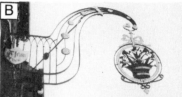

B

C

Above are three hotel signs in Rottweil, situated between the **Schwarzwald** and the **Schwäbische Alb**. Below are the names of the hotels. Which sign goes with which name?

1

2

3

The **Getreidegasse** in Salzburg (on the left) is the most popular shopping street for the thousands of tourists that visit the old town every year. Nearly every shop has a decorative sign outside it. Why is the **Drogerie** (above, in the **Getreidegasse**), called **Mozart Drogerie**?

How can you tell that the sign on the left, outside a **Weinstube** (wine bar) in Weimar, is in East Germany?

In the late 18th and early 19th century, Weimar was a meeting place for writers and thinkers. Goethe and Schiller, two of Germany's most famous writers, lived here. After World War I the **Weimarer Republik** was based there.

Rückblick

- Did you see any decorative signs like those on page 74?
- Did any signs particularly confuse you?

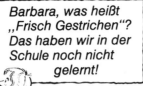

Barbara, was heißt „Frisch Gestrichen"? Das haben wir in der Schule noch nicht gelernt!

Keine Ahnung!

- Did you notice any street signs named after famous people? Which of the people below and on the right
  1 invented the printing press?
  2 was a writer?
  3 was a post-war politician?
  4 were composers?
  5 founded Communism?

- Did any towns you visited have a **Partnerstadt** (twin town)? In which country is the **Partnerstadt** of Vaterstetten, east of Munich?

- Did you notice that cigarette ads warn you about dangers to health, and tell you the quantities of nicotine and tar in the brand?

Wenn du mich in Dortmund besucht hättest, hättest du viele Bierreklamen gesehen!

Dortmund – Bierstadt

German beer, especially from Dortmund and Munich, is famous all over the world. Dortmund produces the second largest quantity of beer in the world (after Milwaukee).

According to a law passed in 1516 only **Malz** (malt), **Hopfen** (hops), **Hefe** (yeast) and **Wasser** (water) may be used to make beer.

Because the Germans don't tilt the glass when they pour a beer, it has much more froth on it than in Britain. It tastes rather like our lager, and is always served chilled.

Ich hoffe, daß sie auch für mich eins haben!

Prost!

It's not just sportsmen and women who enjoy a cool beer …

Final impressions

Compiling an album

When you get back to Britain, put all your thoughts and souvenirs into an album. Arrange them as a diary, a day-by-day account of everything you did and saw. Or divide them into sections, for example *The towns I visited, Transport, The food* (or use the chapter headings of this book).

See you next year

Ich liebe dich!

Auf Wiedersehen!

At one of the lakes in the Sauerland I took a photo of the whole exchange party – Germans and English.

In Salzburg I went to a marvellous ▶ Mozart concert. Mozart was Austrian, and a child prodigy – he played and composed on a tour of Germany, Paris and London when he was only six years old!

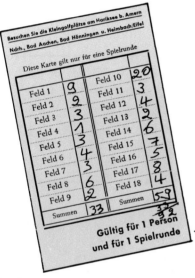

◀ Today we played mini-golf. I was hopeless. Look at my scores!

One day our teachers took us to Dachau, where there was a big concentration camp in the War. It was horrifying walking round the huts and the gas chambers. This statue is a permanent reminder, and a warning that it must never be allowed to happen again.

One day we had a football match against the Germans. Rita and I were great goalkeepers!

Surprise, surprise!

Did you see anything during your stay that surprised you?

This multi-coloured car was spotted in Würzburg. Behind it is the **Residenz** (Bishop's Residence), one of the most impressive Baroque buildings in Germany.

I watched this unusual game of chess.

You see a **Maibaum** (maypole) like this only in the South. This one is in Bavaria, and represents all the local trades.

This sign welcomes ▶ you as you enter Himmelreich, in Austria.

Why do you think this church in Neviges is called the **Skischanze**?

Why does this doctor not inspire you with confidence?

I saw a clown in a tree in Cologne! He was just near the big Gothic cathedral, watching a **Karneval** parade. **Karneval** is a festival celebrated before the beginning of Lent.

Es ist Zeit, ,,Auf Wiedersehen" zu sagen. Hoffentlich kommst du uns bald wieder besuchen. Tschüß!

Alles Guetä! Üf Wiederluege!

Mach's gut! Pfüat di!

FINAL QUIZ

1 Money money money
How much change would you get from a 10 **DM** note if you bought the following:
A a record costing 5,90 **DM**?
B three magazines costing 1,50 **DM** each?
C a bottle of coke costing 1,25 **DM** and a packet of sweets costing 1,10 **DM**?
D a book costing 6,10 **DM** and three comics costing 1,30 **DM** each?
E six rolls costing 12 **Pfennig** each?

2 Drink drink drink
Which of the following statements about drinks are TRUE and which are FALSE?
A Union, Löwenbräu and **DAB** are all brands of beer.
B Schnaps is a mild brew of beer.
C You find the classifications **Kabinett, Spätlese** and **Auslese** on wine bottles.
D The **Oktoberfest** is a big beer festival held every year in Hamburg.

3 Did you see?
You may well have seen the following warning signs. What do they mean?
A KEIN TRINKWASSER
B RAUCHEN VERBOTEN
C HOCHSPANNUNG – LEBENSGEFAHR!
D BITTE DEN RASEN NICHT BETRETEN
E BENUTZUNG AUF EIGENE GEFAHR
F EINBAHNSTRAßE

4 Did you hear?
You may well have heard announcements similar to these. Where would you hear them?
A Haben Sie etwas zu verzollen?
B Achtung! Achtung! Der Zug nach Linz, planmäßige Ankunftszeit 11.30 Uhr, hat voraussichtlich 5 Minuten Verspätung.
C Passagiere des Fluges Nr BA 340 nach Frankfurt werden gebeten, sich zur Paßabfertigung zu begeben.
D Hier ist der norddeutsche Rundfunk mit Nachrichten.
E Kein Anschluß unter dieser Nummer.

5 Look at your maps
All of the following are to be found in German-speaking Europe. Which is the odd one out in each case, and why?
A Heidelberg, Stuttgart, Zürich, Bremen
B Dresden, Kiel, Rostock, Magdeburg
C Innsbruck, Klagenfurt, Graz, Erfurt
D Elbe, Donau, Bayern, Main
E Eiger, Zugspitze, Großglockner, Bodensee

6 What are they?
Below are some famous types of CHEESE, NEWSPAPERS, CARS, MAGAZINES, ELECTRICAL GOODS and CIGARETTES. Which of the above words fits the gap?
A Wartburg and **Trabant** are makes of East German ——.
B Spiegel and **Stern** are both West German ——.
C Salzburger Nachrichten and **Kurier** are Austrian ——.
D Gruyère and **Emmental** are types of Swiss ——.
E HB and **LORD** are brands of West German ——.
F Siemens and **AEG** are West German firms producing ——.

7 Why are they famous?
Here are some famous people from German-speaking countries – but the descriptions do not fit the people. Can you sort them out?
A Paul Klee built one of the first cars.
B Bertold Brecht invented a special type of gas burner.
C Wilhelm Röntgen was a twentieth-century Swiss painter.
D Carl Benz invented a type of engine.
E R.W. Bunsen was a twentieth-century writer.
F Rudolf Diesel invented the X-ray.

8 Read your stars!
Here are the twelve signs of the zodiac – in German and in English. Can you match them up?

LÖWE – WAAGE –WASSERMANN – STIER – SCHÜTZE – FISCHE – WIDDER – KREBS – STEINBOCK – SKORPION – ZWILLINGE – JUNGFRAU

AQUARIUS – PISCES – ARIES – TAURUS – GEMINI – CANCER – LEO – VIRGO – LIBRA – SCORPIO – SAGITTARIUS – CAPRICORN

9 What did you say?

Numbers **i-vi** are things you may well have said whilst you were in Germany; and **A-F** are occasions when you would have said them. Match the right words to the right occasion.

i Ich bin satt.
ii Oh, Verzeihung!
iii Ich bin schrecklich müde.
iv Es tut mir leid, ich hab's eilig.
v Gesundheit!
vi Guten Appetit!

A Your friend has just sneezed.
B You are about to start your meal.
C You are full up.
D You have just trodden on someone's toe.
E You are in a hurry.
F You are nearly asleep.

10 A lot of bottle!

Here's someone's shopping list.. Unfortunately, the containers are rather confused. Can you put the contents in the right container?

EINKAUFSLISTE

1 **Flasche Streichhölzer**
1 **Dose Honig**
1 **Tüte Rotwein**
1 **Schachtel Zucker**
1 **Glas Ochsenschwanzsuppe**

11 What was the sport?

Here are some facts about sporting occasions involving German-speaking countries. Which sport is referred to in each case?

A In the 1986 final West Germany was defeated by Argentina.
B The 1987 world title was won by Peter Müller of Switzerland.
C Berhard Langer first hit the headlines when he climbed a tree to play a shot.
D Steffi Graf won her first Grand Slam title in Paris in 1987.
E Heike Drechsler of East Germany won the 1987 world title with a distance of 7.10 metres.

12 Half and half

Here are the names of eight towns – two each in West Germany, East Germany, Austria and Switzerland. However, the two syllables of each town don't belong together. Can you match up the appropriate first and second syllable, then say which country each of the towns is in?

A Innsburg
B Zürden
C Luzich
D Brebruck

E Leipheim
F Mannmen
G Salzzig
H Dresern

13 Abbreviations

You may well have seen these abbreviations whilst you were abroad. What do they mean?

A DB
B BP
C HBF
D EG
E Vopo

F z.B.
G d.h.
H u.s.w.
I z.Zt.

14 Take your pick

A Kraftwerk is
i a West German pop group
ii a type of West German cheese
iii a cheese factory in West Germany.
B Udo Lindenberg is
i a famous West German warship
ii a famous West German aviator
iii a famous West German pop-singer
C The **Pioniere** and **Freie Deutsche Jugend** are youth groups in
i East Germany
ii West Germany
iii Austria
D The **Reeperbahn** is the centre of the night-life in
i West Berlin
ii Hamburg
iii Munich
E The **Brenner** is
i the Austrian fire-service
ii a type of Austrian coal
iii a mountain pass in Austria

Answers

1 A 4.10 DM, B 5.50 DM, C 7.65 DM, D None, E 9.28 DM. 2 A True, B False, C True, D False. 3 A No drinking water, B No smoking, C High Voltage – Danger!, D Please don't walk on the grass, E At your own risk, F One-way street. 4 A Customs, B Railway station, C Airport, D Radio, E Telephone. 5 A Zürich is in Switzerland and not in W. Germany, B Kiel is in W. Germany and not in the DDR, C Erfurt is in the DDR and not in Austria, D Bayern is a Land, not a river, E The Bodensee is a lake, not a mountain. 6 A Cars, B Magazines, C Newspapers, D Cheese, E Cigarettes, F Electrical goods. 7 A Paul Klee was a twentieth-century Swiss painter, B Bertold Brecht was a twentieth-century writer, C Wilhelm Röntgen invented the X-ray, E R.W. Bunsen invented a special type of gas burner, F Rudolf Diesel invented a type of engine. 8 Löwe = Leo, Waage = Libra, Wassermann = Aquarius, Stier = Taurus, Schütze = Sagittarius, Fische = Pisces, Widder = Aries, Krebs = Cancer, Steinbock = Capricorn, Skorpion = Scorpio, Zwillinge = Gemini, Jungfrau = Virgo. 9 A v, B vi, C i, D ii, E iv, F iii. 10 1 Schachtel Streichhölzer, 1 Glas Honig, 1 Flasche Rotwein, 1 Tüte Zucker, 1 Dose Ochsenschwanzsuppe. 11 A Football, B Downhill skiing, C Golf, D Tennis, E Long jump. 12 A Innsbruck, B Leipzig, C Zürich, D Mannheim, E Salzburg, F Bremen, G Luzern, H Dresden. 13 A Deutsche Bundesbahn, B Bundespost, C Hauptbahnhof – main station, D Europäische Gemeinschaft – Common Market, E Volkspolizist – East German policeman, F z.B. – for example, G d.h. – that is, H und so weiter – etc, I zur Zeit – at the moment. 14 A = i, B = iii, C = i D = ii, E = iii.

79

Answers

Pages 4 & 5
German is also spoken in East Germany, Austria, Switzerland and Liechtenstein. The photo: the Rhine.
1, 2, 3 West Germany: Bonn; flag B; D. East Germany: East Berlin; flag D; DDR. Austria: Vienna; flag C; A. Switzerland: Bern; flag A; CH. Liechtenstein: Vaduz; flag E; FL.
4 Steffi Graf, West Germany: C, Michael Groß, West Germany: E, Heike Drechsler, East Germany: A, Bernhard Langer, West Germany: B, Katharina Witt, East Germany: F, Peter Müller, Switzerland: D. The photo: He was seventeen, and he comes from West Germany.
1 B; West Germany. 2 D; Austria. 3 A; East Germany. 4 C; West Germany. 5 E; East Germany.

Page 11
Bavaria breaks up last for the summer holidays. Baden-Württemberg has extra holidays in February. Hamburg's and Schleswig-Holstein's autumn half-term holiday is longer.

Page 12
There are 100 Pfennig in a Mark, and 100 Groschen in a Schilling.

Page 15
The H stands for Haltestelle.

Page 16
The car is a Porsche from Hamburg. Mercedes 4, Opel 3, Audi 1, BMW 5, Volkswagen 2.

Page 17
The first motorways in Britain were built in 1959. The border on the sign is the East German border. There is petrol, a restaurant, and information at the service station. The recommended speed limit is the one in white on blue, the other two are compulsory ones, the top one for towns and the middle one for the countryside.

Page 18
A and C: rechts, B, D and E: links.

Page 21
1 Munich, 2 Vienna, 3 Salzburg, 4 Hamburg and Dresden, 5 Munich 6 Schubert, Strauss, Lehar, 7 Mozart.

Page 22
A7, B4, C1, D2, E3, F5, G6.

Page 23
The photo: the MZ is an East German motorbike.

Page 26
Mein Vater war ein Wandersmann is called I love to go a-wandering in English. The sign for the shortest hike is the one opposite the hike from Hörde to Hohensyburg. The hike to Herdecke will take five hours. The starting point for the hike to Witten is the youth hostel in Höchsten.
Getreide is corn, Obst is fruit, Weintrauben are grapes, Kartoffeln are potatoes, Gemüse is vegetables and Hopfen are hops.

Page 27
The top label comes from Baden and the bottom one from Rheinhessen.

Page 29
Cochem is on the River Mosel, which is famous for the wine made in the area.
1B, 2E, 3I, 4F, 5C, 6H, 7J, 8D, 9G, 10L, 11A, 12K.

Page 30
Eingang = Entrance. The advertisement is for beer. The photos: you can buy men's and children's shoes; and delicatessen items.

Page 31
A 3rd Floor (Elektro), B Basement (Kosmetik), C 1st floor (Modische Acc.), D Basement (Alles für das Tier), E 4th floor (Café).

Page 32
The sausages are served on pewter plates, with pickled cabbage, horse-radish or potato salad. They are grilled on a beechwood fire.
Suppen A, Eintopf B, Beilagen J, Vom Rind E, Vom Kalb F, Eierspeisen C, Vom Huhn G, Fischgerichte H, Pfannengerichte I, Vom Schwein D.

Page 34
Schnellimbiß means quick snack.

Page 35
The currency is Austrian (Schilling).

Page 38
S = Salzburg, V = Vorarlberg, K = Kärnten, T = Tirol, O = Oberösterreich.

Page 39
The photo: T stand for Tankstelle. Keine Selbstbedienung means No self service. Erfrischungen means Refreshments. You can buy hot drinks.

Page 40
The ÖAMTC and ADAC equivalents are the AA and the RAC.

Page 46
1 Außenministerium, 2 Deutsches Theater

Page 47
Hameln = Hamlin, and is famous for the Pied Piper.
Müllmanner 5, Taxifahrerin 2, Pflastermaler 7, Straßenmusikanten 3, Lokführer 1, Polizist 6, Straßenverkäufer 4.

Page 48
Adidas and Puma are the most famous German makes.

Page 51
Ochsenbraten is also called Rinderbraten. Würzfleisch comes from poultry. Gulasch originates from Hungary.
1 A East Germany, B West Germany, C Austria. 2 Salzburg. 3 A ship. 4 Rodenkirchen, near Cologne.

Page 53
1 Bratwurst, 2 Teller, 3 Reis, 4 Suppe, 5 Eier, 6 Rotkohl, 7 Linsen, 8 Nuss, 9 Steak, 10 Kakao, 11 Omelett, 12 Tomaten, 13 Nudel, 14 Lachs, 15 Saft, 16 Trauben, 17 Niere, 18 Eintopf, 19 Fisch, 20 Huhn. Vertical word: Brot. The photo: from Leipzig, East Germany.

Page 54
Abbreviated subjects: Latein, Französisch, Mathematik, Katholische Religion. This pupil is Catholic.

Page 55
The class had Geography, Maths, Art, German and Religion. One pupil was ill.

Page 57
Meißen is famous for china. Cigarette ads do carry a health warning.

Page 58
Emergency doctor on duty: 55 86 61. Chemist on Saturday: 670 40 50 or 40 43 41. The Telefonseelsorge is like the British Samaritans. Suchtgefährdete are drug addicts.

Page 59
Rezepteinwurf is where you post your prescription, and Nachtglocke is night-time bell.
The Salbe can be inhaled or rubbed in. You should take ½ – 1 teaspoon of the medicine, once a day in the evening.

Page 61
Football is played at regional level because distances are great and travel costs high. Essen is the largest city without a first division team. The column headings stand for Spiele (games played), Gewonnen (won), Unentschieden (tie), Verloren (lost), Tore (goals), Differenz (goal difference) and Punkte (points). FC stands for Fußballclub. München is in Bavaria. There are two points for a win.
Karl-Heinz Rummenigge's brother is called Michael. His team is first in the Tabelle.

Page 63
The programmes are on Sunday. It's a news programme. There are four films, two German, one Russian and one American. ZDF stands for Zweites Deutsches Fernsehen. The news programme on the 2nd channel is called heute. The film is about training animals. Kinderkino is for children.

Page 65
Austrian Schlag = German Schlagsahne.

Page 66
Schneeketten are used to get a grip in snow and ice. The car is an Audi.

Page 67
The photos: Ausfahrt = Motorway exit, Umleitung = Diversion, Autobahndreieck = Motorway merger, Unfall = Accident.
1 Rose, 2 Nase, 3 Hase, 4 Mond, 5 Dose, 6 Brite, 7 Leber, 8 Name, 9 Ulm, 10 Hans.

Page 68
Six objects: Heft, Buch, Lineal, Radiergummi, Kuli, Bleistift. Subjects: Englisch, Kunst, Physik, Deutsch, Chemie, Sport, Geschichte, Mathematik, Biologie, Erdkunde.

Page 71
The liver sausage is made from calf's liver. The peanuts cost 2.39 DM for 250 grams. The Salat is made from herring.

Page 72
The photo: the Bodensee = Lake Constance.

Page 73
The Salzkammergut is in Austria. The zoo entrance prices are given in East German Marks.

Page 74
Mozart was born in Salzburg. The sign has HO on it (see page 30).

Page 75
1 Gutenberg, 2 Schiller, 3 Adenauer, 4 Strauss and Offenbach, 5 Marx and Engels. The Partnerstadt of Vaterstetten is in France.